AF386869

"As an autistic person, the message I received from the world was clear—'there's something wrong with you.' Sean's book offers a different narrative. Not one of immutable conditions, but of an evolving self capable of cultivating flexibility and self-compassion. Sean shows us that much of the behavior we commonly associate with autism can be understood (and improved) by taking the state of our nervous system into account. If you often feel stuck, rigid, anxious, or incapable of connection, this accessible introduction to Polyvagal Theory provides a practical starting point."

—**Paul Micallef,** creator of *Autism From The Inside*, YouTube channel

Neural Exercises for Autism

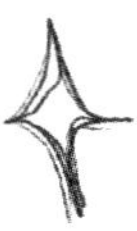

Neural Exercises for Autism

Embracing Your
Capacity for Flexibility,
Connection, and Joy

Sean Inderbitzen

Norton Professional Books

An Imprint of W. W. Norton & Company
Independent Publishers Since 1923

Chapter illustrations by Grace Boardman

Copyright © 2026 by Sean Inderbitzen

For information about permission to reproduce selections from this book, write to
Permissions, W. W. Norton & Company, Inc., 500 Fifth Avenue, New York, NY 10110

For information about special discounts for bulk purchases, please contact
W. W. Norton Special Sales at specialsales@wwnorton.com or 800-233-4830

Manufacturing by Versa Press
Book design by THE COSMIC LION
Production manager: Gwen Cullen

ISBN: 978-1-324-08289-7 (Paperback)

W. W. Norton & Company, Inc., 500 Fifth Avenue, New York, NY 10110
www.wwnorton.com

W. W. Norton & Company Ltd., 15 Carlisle Street, London W1D 3BS

Authorized EU representative: EAS, Mustamäe tee 50, 10621 Tallinn, Estonia

1 2 3 4 5 6 7 8 9 0

To my boys,

To my youngest, you are always enough even when you lose. You might not always be the best at everything, but you will always be the best at being Bo. And I hope you know how deeply wonderful he is. To my eldest, you don't have to try so hard to be enough. You just are, and it's not a race. Enjoy the trip and the rocks from all the weird places you go: Pennsylvania, California, and more. I can't wait to see where you find them.

Jordyn,

Even though we don't talk much anymore, I consistently remember the sense of warmth your presence brings. That warmth still lights me inside up and soothes the dark corners of my heart. Please don't stop.

Mitchell and Kaitlyn,

I'm so glad to have family like you. You consistently protect me, and make me celebrate birthdays I begrudgingly attend, even though I secretly am superbly grateful for. It is not lost on me how big your hearts are, and I hope you find all the warmth and joy the universe has.

Josh,

Dude, if I have one call from prison you are the person I'm calling. I'm glad to know you and I cherish all the feedback you give. Sometimes it's what I want to hear and other times it's not; either way it's always needed.

Christopher,

You have such passion for helping people and a desire to create a better world for everyone you come in contact with. I'm always such a fan of your passion for being innovative, bringing quality into the way we help autists and other humans alike. To you there is no difference; good service is good service. Keep at that. It's catchy.

Steve,

I can always count on some loyal opposition and Norwegian perspective from you. But like you always say, people at their heart are good, and as we say on our phone calls, world peace is not that far away. Love you dude.

Cindy,

I'm ever bemused by the way our journeys spiral. It's fun getting to walk on a parallel path with you, and I love seeing the way your life unfolds.

Brent,

You always call me Dr. Inderbitzen. I hate that. But I enjoy it when you do it because it reminds me how much you appreciate the work I've done to get here.

Jim,
Our talks are short, but generally arrive at useful and profound decisions. Clarity has always been my friend with you.

Jason,
I learn a lot from your mentorship, so much so that I find myself asking people, "How can you be the most you in this moment if we simply release the outcome?" Thanks for taking a chance on me and sharing how much you mean to me.

Danielle,
In my mind there will always be before you and after you. Before you I saw myself as a monster and so desperately longed for love. After you, I can look in the mirror and smile at who I see. He's not as scary, hairy, or full of fangs. No, he stands three feet tall, has curls, a grin, and a smirk. He doesn't need much. He just knows Christ loves him. Thank you for not seeing me as my worst moments. I can't forget this.

To the women I've written about in this book,
I feel like Vanity Fair *said it best: Boyfriends are embarrassing. I know in our short or lengthy interactions, I probably did something or said something really stupid. That is not lost on me. Sending you love and light.*

Contents

Acknowledgments

Admittedly this book was never one I particularly wanted to write. It came as a request from someone who presented it to me and at first I said let me think on it. I consulted my usual cohort of advisors, if you will, and unintentionally they all agreed. Much to my chagrin they expressed how God had given me a gift in all this pain.

As my favorite Lang Leav quote goes, "I know you have seen things you wish you hadn't. You have done things you wish you could take back. And you wonder why you were thrown into the thick of it all—why you had to suffer the way you did. And as you are sitting there alone and hurting, I wish I could put a pen in your hand and gently remind you how the world has given you poetry and now you must give it back." I forget this sometimes, that pain is a gift, and suffering is an inkwell; gifting us with stories to write, teach, and impart lessons that came at a cost.

For me this work is one I did in service of a divine call, and really is a faithful response to that. It was a calling that I didn't want, but one which has called me into growth. To become big enough to admit my imperfection and see it with kind eyes. To make sense of this, let me offer you both an image and a story. In 2023, on my left shoulder, I got a tattoo of a little girl, probably no more than 5 years old, kissing a large wolf, who is aggressively uncomfortable from the affection. Up until September of 2025, I always identified with the wolf in the tattoo. Ugly, aggressive, a bit impulsive, and unkempt. But then I had an encounter with a person who she saw me not as the wolf, but the little girl. Recognizing me, all my pain, all my scars, all my rough edges; she saw all of this. Knowing and witnessing how arguably messed up I am, she still found a way to see me as the little girl.

While this person was only passing through, I've been unable go back to witnessing myself as a monster. Instead I now understand what she saw. A little boy, who is totally and completely unaware of the evil the world holds, and able to tune into the feelings and experiences of others. And for that I am forever grateful. With this in mind I invite you to partake in my pain. So that you too may begin to see that you are not a monster, but a little human being. Because you are in fact a blessing, not a burden. This is your invitation to see that.

Author's Note

There is an ongoing conversation within the neurodiversity community about whether autism should be treated as an identity or as a disorder. This discussion places those who want to be of help (social workers, physicians, psychiatrists, researchers) in the challenging position of identifying which is the politically correct stance. As an advocate of the polyvagal perspective on autism, I'd like to take time to discuss both sides of the argument and to offer a third perspective, one from the lens of personality, as developed by the Personality Development Group and Daniel Siegel, MD. This perspective is rooted in the field of interpersonal neurobiology and the evolutionary biology work of the late Jaak Panksepp, PhD. As an Autist, I invite readers to consider, with openness and curiosity, the validity of each of these perspectives, understanding that everyone will arrive at their own conclusions. This book is written from a perspective that is consistent with the field of interpersonal neurobiology—an interdisciplinary framework that draws on concepts from psychology, neuroscience, and other fields to explore how the mind and mental well-being are impacted by interpersonal relationships.

While other perspectives, such as Richard Schwartz's parts theory, might be considered valuable contributions to this discussion, I have made a conscious choice to exclude these perspectives because this book is oriented toward interpersonal neurobiology. The distinction between Daniel Siegel's theory of personality and Schwartz's theory of parts lies in the fact that Siegel considers parts of the self to be verbs (i.e., malleable over time), which I, as a writer, find more compelling than Schwartz's notion that parts of the self are nouns (i.e., static). This distinction, while simple, goes beyond the present neurodiversity discussion by moving beyond psychodynamic theory and is consistent with a view of the self as a whole, composed of many parts.

When people say, "This is my Autist self"—in other words, that autism is a facet of their identity—I find I have a rather strong reaction. As someone who has never had the privilege of finding advantage in my autism, my journey has been largely trial by fire, regardless of whether I label my autism as an identity or a disorder. But as one of my clinical mentors and fellow interpersonal neurobiology (IPNB) authors, Pat Ogden, PhD, offered me, "If people define themselves using only a single word, they must find some benefit to it" (P. Ogden, personal communication, November 10, 2024). In short, there must be a reason why some people find benefit in embracing autism as their identity. So, I consulted with a number of experts who identify as Autists regarding what benefits they see in embracing the label. Our personal communications made it clear that the greatest benefit of adopting autism as an identity appears to be the ability to find connection with other oppressed voices and the ability to remain a critic of the challenges Autists face.

Critics of the identity perspective—those who are in favor of using the word "disorder" to describe autism—perceive autism as a lifelong experience of restrictive, repetitive patterns of interest or behavior along with deficits in social skills. Those who are in the identity camp criticize the use of "disorder" because they feel that it stigmatizes and discriminates in a way that systematically oppresses those with this neurotype. The challenge that comes with embracing autism as a lifelong, enduring identity is what to do with the countless children and adults with autism who seek to become more flexible, open, and creative and more connected to those with different neurotypes.

In my eyes, proponents of the identity view miss this challenge—the real and powerful suffering people experience as a result of their autism—entirely. Proponents of the identity view in the neurodiversity conversation may consider this challenge to be the result of internalized ableism (Autistic folks' absorption of negative beliefs about neuroatypical tendencies). In the end, whether you consider autism through a disorder or an identity lens, both views are relatively pessimistic when it comes to the potential for relief from suffering. Enter the polyvagal perspective on autism, which is consistent with neither of these perspectives; Polyvagal Theory posits a much more optimistic outlook on change than either of these other perspectives can. Polyvagal Theory proposes a neurobiological way for mapping the evolutionary relationship between mind and body onto three distinct branches of the nervous system: the ventral vagal system, the sympathetic system, and the dorsal vagal system. Each system serves a different function: The dorsal system serves to induce shutdown responses (think of an opossum playing dead; activation of this branch might cause you to feel numb or to dissociate). The sympathetic system is in charge of initiating fight-or-flight responses (imagine a gazelle running from a lion; activation of this branch might cause you to feel anxiety, panic, or rage). The ventral system enables social functions (when this branch of our nervous system is activated, we feel at ease and can form bonds with others).

From a polyvagal lens, feeling "stuck" and disconnected from others—both hallmark experiences of autism—may be considered the result of a nervous system whose dorsal and sympathetic branches are activated. Imagine, for instance, an Individualized Education Plan (IEP) meeting: the teacher might raise concerns about a child with autism, and if that teacher uses an activating word, it might be enough to evoke a rigid response from the child. The child's apparent unwillingness to engage in the meeting might actually reflect a sympathetic fight response, in which the child's body is remembering the emotional experience of that activating word. The memory might evoke hostility from the child in the form of anger, short responses, folded arms, grunting, spitting, and perhaps even profanities. By dismissing the role the autonomic nervous system plays for this child, the administrators and other adults may assume the child is stubborn and think the child is consciously choosing to be defiant. Thus, an IEP team may become overly preoccupied with the child's angry response to a teacher's recommendation rather than exploring ways to partner with the child, who may have thoughts that they are unable to successfully communicate, such as, "This teacher has no idea what I need; if only she would *hear* me." The IEP team may also be unaware that the experience of feeling unheard is stacking on top of memories of times the student felt bullied by their peers, thus eliciting a response that comes across as hostile.

Regardless of the child's diagnosis, the rigidity described in the scenario above inhibits the child's connection with their team members. From a polyvagal lens, the child is considered to be existing in a highly dorsal state (i.e., shut down or in a state of collapse). Concurrent with the triggered anger, the child's heart beats quickly, and so the child simultaneously experiences a sympathetic state (i.e., activated or "fight" mode). Thus, from a polyvagal perspective, the individual with autism may experience reduced access to their ventral vagal system and a greater tendency toward sympathetic arousal and/or dorsal withdrawal. These states are not inherent traits; they can be modulated with experiences that support neuroception of safety. And while being rigid (like incredible attention to detail or a fascination with a specific topic or interest) can have its advantages, it certainly has a coequal set of disadvantages. However, my belief—the perspective from which this book is written—is that, as Autists, we have the capability to modulate our experience. By reducing activation of the dorsal and sympathetic branches of our autonomic nervous systems, we can reduce rigidity and increase our capacity for social connection. This is the goal of the neural exercises presented in this book: to promote a more flexible and deeper connection with others as we emote, think, and remember. I include the following poem, "A love letter to my masked self," by Jacqueline Jebian Garcia, because it captures so deeply the reconciliation of us to us. The process of reconciliation is often however fraught with remorse, regret, and the pain of a heartfelt apology. I hear that and see that in Jacqueline's words, which is why I feel it is so important to share with you.

A love letter to my masked self
By Jacqueline Jebian Garcia, MS, CCC-SLP

To the masked version of me:

I write to you with trembling hands and an open heart.

*You—the one who walked the world with an
invisible weight, unsure why it all felt so hard.
You—the one who became fluent in the
language of fitting in.
You—the one who built safety by blending in,
by pleasing, by hiding, by masking.*

*I see now how much love lived inside your
survival.*

*Before I became a mother, you thought your
differences were flaws.*

AUTHOR'S NOTE

You traded authenticity for acceptance,
because that's what the world demanded of
you.

But you were never broken.
You were masked—not because you lacked
truth, but because the world wasn't ready for it.

Then came the children.
The ones who would crack open the silence you
had learned to live within.
The ones who would reflect back to me the very
things you buried.
The ones who helped me remember who we
were before the forgetting.

Because of them, I met you again.
And this time I didn't turn away.

Now I can feel the parts of you I once tried to
outgrow—but now hold like sacred roots.

I am unlearning. And in my unlearning, I am
embodying liberation. Because I am now safe enough.

Neural Exercises for Autism

1
..

Where to Begin?

Technical civilization is man's conquest of space. It is a triumph frequently achieved by sacrificing an essential ingredient of existence, namely, time. In technical civilization we expend time to gain space.

—ABRAHAM JOSHUA HESCHEL, *THE SABBATH*

Daniel Siegel believes the self to be an emergent property; that is, the self emerges across the planes of time, space, and possible outcomes (Siegel, 2024b). According to this theory, the self is "emergent" in the sense that it is a thing that is not yet complete. Some readers may find this notion disturbing—the idea that you, as a self, do not exist as a static entity.

This is a wild proposition: that you are not complete, and yet you are fully you. While the field of physics lends weight to this possibility, positing that humans are patterns of energy and potential for the creation of energy, in psychology literature, this possibility is largely absent from discussions of the self. Thinkers like Richard Schwartz talk about parts of self as if they are things that can be nailed down and defined. For instance, Schwartz (1995) states,

A part is not just a temporary emotional state or habitual thought pattern. Instead, it is a discrete and autonomous mental system that has an idiosyncratic range of emotion, style of expression, set of abilities, desires, and view of the world.

Schwartz's view of the self as a whole comprised of parts is deeply validating and saved my life (Klein & Gangi, 2010; Eve et al., 2023; Ribáry et al., 2017; Brenner et al., 2023; Hacohen et al., 2019; Schiepek et al., 2016). However, as I continue to grow, learn, and encounter more people, I find myself gravitating to the argument presented by Dan Siegel in his most recent work, *Personality and Wholeness in Therapy*, that self is a *verb* rather than a noun (in other words, parts of the self are changeable rather than static). I have encountered this malleability within my own experience of rigidity and social disconnection; these rigid parts of me are not static but transient. My capacity for flexibility and social connection shifts over time.

In this book, the word *Self*, with a capital *S*, refers to the multiple and consistent adaptive strategies that present as patterns of emoting, thinking, and behaving across time and contexts (Klein & Gangi, 2010; Eve et al., 2023; Ribáry et al., 2017;

Brenner et al., 2023; Hacohen et al., 2019; Schiepek et al., 2016). If we apply Siegel's lens of the emergent Self to autism, we begin to see autism as an experience rather than a label. This can perhaps be best explained using Stephen W. Porges's Polyvagal Theory. In this chapter, we will answer the following questions: What is Polyvagal Theory? How do we define autism as an *experience rather than a label*? And can we modify that experience through neural exercises?

WHAT IS POLYVAGAL THEORY?

Polyvagal Theory was created by Stephen Porges, who in his *Pocket Guide to Polyvagal Theory* writes, "According to Polyvagal Theory, the face–heart connection provides humans and other mammals with an integrated social engagement system that detects and projects features of 'safety'" (2017, p. 27). Polyvagal experts such as Deb Dana, and Arielle Schwartz often begin explanations of Polyvagal Theory by describing the vagus nerve as the "wandering nerve" (Dana, 2021). These experts are referring to the fact that the vagus nerve is organized into (or "wanders" into) three sections: the ventral vagal system, the sympathetic nervous system, and the dorsal vagal system. The dorsal vagal system evolved first, in our amphibian ancestors, followed by the sympathetic nervous system and, finally, the ventral vagal system. I find that the best way to unpack the functions of these three systems is through a series of stories and by revisiting the original theorists' words to capture both the depth and intuitive simplicity of Polyvagal Theory.

Dorsal Vagal System

If you listen closely to a virtual talk I once gave to an audience of other psychotherapists, you can hear a series of clunks, smacks, and thuds in the background. These were the sounds of the drawers in my bedroom slamming shut, and the reason they were slamming shut is because my partner had decided to leave our relationship that afternoon. And I, in my ever-dorsal way, shut off the desire to chase my partner down and continued my presentation to a Zoom call attended by several thousand people. In the eyes of the organization for which I was presenting, it's one of the better talks I've given, but I'm not sure any amount of accolades or money can really make up for my not chasing after my partner.

If you watch me closely in the recording of this presentation, you might notice that though I'm talkative and seemingly engaged with the audience, my eyes are wandering. This was because I was functioning on autopilot; I was dissociating, completely disconnected from any feelings. My mind was so gone, so collapsed, that I was unable to show up for myself nor this part of myself that wanted to chase after my partner. This is a prime example of the dorsal system in action; it's the oldest branch of the autonomic nervous system and is responsible for shutting down the body in an effort to conserve energy (Székely, 2000). Consider an opossum playing dead in an attempt to evade a predator—this is also the dorsal system in action, and it's necessary for the opossum's survival. But in humans, the dorsal branch has evolved to collapse the mind in a way that can be unhelpful, as it did in this personal experience with my partner.

The Sympathetic System

Let's take another example from my own life to explore the sympathetic branch of the autonomic nervous system. Imagine a young man, 18, pretty hot-headed and, dare I say, stubborn. As he drives to school one day, he goes too quickly around a turn in the road. With his eyes locked on his rearview mirror, he veers into oncoming traffic and—*thud*—a red bumper goes spinning into the air, and the oncoming car goes into the ditch on the other side of the road. The young man, however, just keeps going. And going. And going. A few minutes later, he finds himself sitting in the school parking lot.

On the sympathetic system, Porges writes, "When our autonomic system is overwhelmed by our sympathetic nervous system, we, in a sense, become skittish. We'll aggressively hit others, and we'll misinterpret others' cues" (Porges, 2017). The sympathetic system—or fight-or-flight response—manages the functions of the nervous system responsible for escaping or challenging a perceived threat. In other words, the sympathetic nervous system is responsible for readying our muscles for fighting off or fleeing from danger. Like our mammalian ancestors who were chased by predators on the savannah, I, too, followed my prehistoric urge and took off from the scene of a car accident. "I" was gone, replaced by "prehistoric Sean." When this powerful, primeval drive took over, I was unable to be flexible or face uncertainties about my future.

Ventral Vagal System

The younger of my two sons is named Ralph, after the timelessly great Ralph Lauren. Much like his namesake, Ralph is incredibly intuitive and is also one of the sweetest eight-year-old boys you will ever meet. He's often sensitive, like his father, and has a need to be close. He loves to cuddle and will often ask if he can cuddle with me at night. Unlike his older brother, Shean, Ralph is still small enough to fit right into my chest; he is the perfect height for snuggling and staying warm.

I love these moments of being his father, and they are also a great illustration of the most recently evolved branch of the nervous system: the ventral branch, more commonly known as the parasympathetic system. This system is known as the rest-and-digest system and mediates all the cues of safety and sociality, allowing for things like cuddles, snuggles, eye contact, and more. When this system is activated, we experience flexibility and availability for connection. And in this magical space, we begin to see a whole series of possible ways we might become more flexible in our emoting, thinking, and remembering, and, in turn, to develop deeper and more meaningful connections. As Porges says, "Safety is critical in enabling humans to optimize their potential along several domains. Safe states are a prerequisite not only for social behavior but also for accessing higher brain structures that enable humans to be creative and generative" (Porges, 2017).

AN EXPERIENCE VERSUS A DIAGNOSIS

Autism was first included as a possible diagnosis in the third edition of the *Diagnostic and Statistical Manual of Mental Disorders* (*DSM-III*), published in 1980, and emerged from thinkers like Hans Asperger and Leo Kanner, whose works described autism in the 1940s (Asperger, 1944; Kanner, 1968). The *DSM-5-TR*, published in 2019, describes autism in two ways: (1) restrictive, repetitive patterns of interest and behaviors, and (2) failure to grasp social communication effectively. In *Autism in Polyvagal Terms*, I describe being an Autist as being mentally inflexible and experiencing a decreased sense of social engagement. Viewed through a polyvagal lens, Autistic traits may, in part, reflect a nervous system pattern where sympathetic arousal or dorsal inhibition dominates over ventral vagal regulation. This dysregulation does not define the condition but offers a lens for understanding how environment, stimuli, sensations, and internal cues of safety—or their absence—shape behavior (I will discuss this further in later chapters). Around 14 studies, conducted over 5 decades, by independent researchers reflect a significant correlation between autism and higher levels of heart rate. While there is a great deal more to be said about this, I recommend readers read *Autism in Polyvagal Terms* to understand Autism can be impairing. It can just as easily be a strength; however, in my eyes, it being a strength is largely state-dependent and, as I have said, requires the ability to self-regulate. Thus, while being diagnosed with autism is not a death sentence, as Ole Ivar Lovaas once described it in a *New York Times* article on March 10, 1987 (Goleman, 1987), living with autism can be challenging to one's experiences of emoting, thinking, and remembering (not to mention the challenges to one's sensory experiences, but we will discuss that in a later chapter).

Despite very real impairments that can present in autism, it can be helpful to consider autism as an experience rather than a diagnosis or label. The term "experiential" carries with it Siegel's notion of the Self as an emergent entity. That is, to call autism "experiential" is to define it in part as a state-dependent reflection of the autonomic nervous system, which is dynamic and context dependent. Autism is alive, present, and transitory. Personality, as Siegel (2024) defines it, is "persistent patterns of emotion, thinking and behavior that exist across times and contexts"—a definition that could easily be applied to autism. Like personality, autism is an emergent quality; it is not a state of being that is fixed, but rather a propensity to emote, think, and remember in ways that are rigid and disconnected from both oneself and others. This disconnection or alienation from oneself and others represents the very crux of the issue that I address in this work. How can we transform our emoting, thinking, and remembering from inflexible and alienating ways to more flexible and connecting ways? The answer is surprisingly simple: neural exercises.

WHAT ARE NEURAL EXERCISES?

The neural exercises I present in this book are practices, rooted in applied neuroscience, that increase social connectedness and decrease inflexibility in emoting, thinking, remembering, and sensing the world. These practices were designed to build what I term *vagal efficiency* (Inderbitzen, 2024). For me, vagal efficiency (as it will be used in this book, not as the metric used in research papers) refers to the nervous system's ability to shift flexibly from states of defense (sympathetic or dorsal) to a regulated state of safety and social engagement (ventral vagal). This concept builds on Polyvagal Theory's emphasis on state regulation and heart–brain dynamics. Much like building inner musculature, vagal efficiency can be built by repeating neural exercises, allowing for greater connection and increased mental flexibility. Throughout the work, I refer to these exercises as *flipping the vagal switch*. To promote the practice of these neural exercises, space is provided at the end of each chapter for you to unpack and work through each exercise.

Neuroscientific approaches that are rooted in the concepts of cultivating safety, sensorimotor psychotherapy, mindfulness, social work pedagogy, motivational interviewing, and biofeedback are integrated into these neural exercises. These interventions have been shown to decrease rigidity and increase social connectedness and are most effective when applied along with a certain set of values, which have been shown to drive change. These values are *kindness, quality, openness, generosity, respect, organicity,* and *mindfulness,* and it is the application of these values that allows the neural exercises to be successful. Neural exercises alone can be interesting and helpful, but the values or attitudes applied while practicing these exercises are the key to creating real psychological change. This is evident, for example, in well-studied practices like Acceptance and Commitment Therapy and motivational interviewing, both of which rest on values like the ones embodied in this work. Considering the values presented alongside each exercise will become increasingly important as you make your way through this book, for if these attitudes are not developed, the interventions are less likely to be helpful.

1 **Kindness:** Responding in the gentlest and easiest way we can, achieved by being attuned to our own autonomic nervous system and the autonomic nervous system of others

2 **Quality:** Excellence, reliability, ethics, integrity, professionalism, responsiveness to emerging evidence (MINT, n.d.)

3 **Openness:** Evolving, emergent, open-minded, innovative, flexible, expanding the boundaries, growth, humility, curiosity, self-reflective (MINT, n.d.)

4 **Generosity:** Nonpossessiveness, sharing, acknowledging, collaborating, cooperating, giving more than you receive (MINT, n.d.)

5 **Respect:** Valuing individual and professional diversity; demonstrating internationality, kindness, listening, communication, egalitarianism (MINT, n.d.)

6 **Organicity:** The internal wisdom of all living systems; the healing power and intelligence that is within; the unique, mysterious, and emergent growth path within each of us that the therapist nurtures (Sensorimotor Psychotherapy Institute, 2022)

7   **Mindfulness:** Encouraging present-moment awareness of both client and therapist experiences, calling attention to this present-moment awareness (this principle is likely useful only if it is as self-directed and concerned with transference as it is other-directed)

PULLING IT ALL TOGETHER

It is my hope that in the pages of this book you will find the tools, values, and skills you need to flip your own vagal switch and live a richer and deeper human experience. With more flexibility, you'll likely find that your range of emoting expands, your thinking becomes less prison-like, and your memory recall becomes less dysregulating. And with more connection, you may discover deeper feelings of connectedness, develop the propensity to see and trust the best in others, and, hopefully, remember why you set out to do this work: to enjoy a more expansive Autist life.

2

Autism Through the Lens of Polyvagal Theory

> Wholeness can be experienced in a world of actualization arising from a sea of potential—what we name "a plane of possibility."
>
> —DANIEL SIEGEL AND THE PDP GROUP, *PERSONALITY AND WHOLENESS IN THERAPY*

As I mentioned in my author's note, there is an ongoing debate around whether to call autism a *disorder* or an *identity*. While the American Psychiatric Association has defined it as a disorder for nearly 44 years, neurodiversity advocates like Judy Singer have been calling it an identity since 1998, the time she is also credited with coining the term *neurodiversity*. In recent years there has been a strong push for viewing autism as an identity, with thinkers like social psychologist Devon Price promoting this view in his 2022 book *Unmasking Autism,* in which he argues that it is the neurotypical world, not those with autism, that must change. While this argument is certainly popular, it rests on the idea that identity is "a subjective sense of an invigorating sameness and continuity. . . . It is the person's feeling of being a distinct and integrated individual who is recognized and accepted by others" (Erikson, 1950, p. 25). This definition—originally posed in 1968 by psychoanalyst Erik Erikson in his book *Identity: Youth and Crisis*—fails to take into account the role of attachment on human development, which ultimately leads to the development of certain patterns of emoting, thinking, and recalling memories, as well as the role of state-specific activation across the human nervous system—all of which affect how we interact with the world. Relegating autism to an identity, then, fundamentally discounts what modern neuroscience teaches about formation of the Self.

I've mentioned that this book is written from an interpersonal neurobiology perspective—that is, it is written through the lens of an interdisciplinary field of study that draws on various disciplines to understand the relationship between attachment and human development. So, what can we come to understand about the Self through this framework? What exactly is a polyvagal model of autism, and when does it present as disordering? This chapter will address these crucial questions and will explain what bottom-up processing is. Beginning with the body and working our way up to emotions and cognitions provides a valuable way of shifting what are arguably disordered ways of functioning as an Autist. Finally, we will discuss how, by adopting this polyvagal model of autism, we can move from disordered states of being to more flexible and connected ways of being by flipping the vagal switch via a series of neural exercises.

WHAT IS THIS THING CALLED THE SELF?

As mentioned in Chapter 1, in this book the Self is considered to be *the multiple and consistent adaptive strategies that present as patterns of emoting, thinking, and behaving across time and contexts* (Klein & Gangi, 2010; Eve et al., 2023; Ribáry et al., 2017; Brenner et al., 2023; Hacohen et al., 2019; Schiepek et al., 2016). This definition builds on Siegel's definition of personality, "persistent patterns of emotion, thinking and behavior that exist across time and contexts" (Siegel, 2024a), as defined in his book *Personality and Wholeness in Therapy*. While this work does not delve into the discussion of parts of the self as richly as some others do, such as those of Pat Ogden or Richard Schwartz, Siegel does make the key distinction of viewing the self as a verb. That is, when we consider our identity as Erikson posits—"a collection of characteristics that guide behavior and create a sense of continuity and uniqueness" (Siegel, 2024)—we must do so through the lens of time, because humans are unfolding experiences, not static objects.

In this departure from more traditional definitions of the self, it is impossible not to acknowledge the role of Richard Schwartz in forming this dynamic definition through his development of the Internal Family Systems (IFS) model. Schwartz, relying on evidence from neuroscience (for more, see Schwartz, 1995, 2020, 2023a, 2023b, and his own clinical work), sees the self as multiple rather than singular, another departure from Eriksonian and earlier psychoanalytic thought on the self. Schwartz argues that personality can be broken down into multiple *parts*, each with distinct characteristics that fall under three categories: *exiles, protectors,* and *managers.*

Parts are subpersonalities that have their "own feelings, perceptions, beliefs, motivations and memories" (Weiss, 2013, p. 1). In Internal Family Systems, these are considered nouns, whereas here we view them as verbs.

Exiles are "young child part[s] that [are] carrying pain from the past" (Weiss, 2013, p. 1).

Protectors are subpersonalities that try "to block off pain that is arising inside you or protect you from hurtful incidents or distressing relationships in your current life" (Weiss, 2013, p. 1).

Managers are "protector[s] that [try] to proactively arrange your life and your psyche so that the pain of Exiles does not come to the surface" (Weiss, 2013, p. 1).

The key distinction I make in this text is that, like in an applied neural exercise (ANE) framework, the Self living with autism is comprised of parts that are dynamic—subpersonalities that are ever changing but orient themselves much like exiles, managers, and protectors. Schwartz, on the other hand, views these parts as nouns (static), and they are treated in the IFS model as discrete, rather than evolving. I like to use a metaphor to help describe what I would call a "fixer part" (similar to a manager). My clients often cite these particular subpersonalities as acting like someone in a helping profession (such as a nurse or social worker) whose primary job function is to "repair," "make better," or "prevent harm." Let's take the example of a social worker: In the specific role and context of the social worker's job, their willingness and ability to continue working with someone who drinks excessively is what we'd call *adaptive* (that is, it helps the social worker be successful at their job). But when the social worker exhibits the same behavior in a different context—for example, a romantic relationship—that behavior becomes *maladaptive* (harmful). In a romantic relationship context, it is *adaptive* to hold a boundary and say to their partner, "I cannot tolerate your drinking; and if you can't stop, I'm out." If the social worker is unwilling to walk away from a dysfunctional relationship, this is *maladaptive*. Again, the strategy of "fixing" is adaptive in one context (substance counseling) and maladaptive in another (a romantic relationship).

We use the term *strategies* (rather than characteristics) in ANE because they describe behaviors that may at one point have been adaptive ways to survive but have become maladaptive in the current circumstances. Much the same as our fictional social worker's strategy of "fixing" those around her, we all have subpersonalities that may have developed strategies for "fixing" us or "preventing harm." At some point, in some context, these strategies genuinely did help us or prevent harm (they were adaptive); but now, they may be *causing* us harm (they've become maladaptive).

The ANE definition of Self also draws from the field of Sensorimotor Psychotherapy and the work of Pat Ogden and her predecessor Ron Kurtz (another pioneer in the field of somatic psychology), creator of the Hakomi Method. In her work, Ogden uses a strengths view of the body's expression of parts in terms of what she refers to as *adaptive strategies* rather than using the language of parts. An adaptive strategy "is an ecological approach that addresses the relationship of a person with their surroundings" (Sensorimotor Psychotherapy Institute, 2023). For our purposes an adaptive strategy is a pattern by which parts of oneself attempt to help the individual survive a situation—in one context, the strategy may be helpful, but in another it may be maladaptive. Within the ANE frame, the term *adaptive strategy* is used to describe a function of a part in its efforts to survive. Again, along the plane of possibilities, these strategies are expressed in the form of energetic expressions in emoting, thinking, and recalling in ways that protect, manage, or hold pain. In people with autism, these somatic, emotive, cognitive, and internal sensations and movements tend to become rigidly organized.

While each theory addresses bits and pieces of the definition presented for the Self in this text, the exercises throughout this book draw on all three perspectives to develop in those who use them the capacity for deeper and more meaningful connection. As we cultivate ways to be more connected and increasingly flexible by flipping the vagal switch via the application of neural exercises, we will continually encounter pieces of each of these psychotherapeutic practices. Now that this view of the Self has been established, I will turn the discussion to why and how we can view autism in polyvagal terms.

AUTISM IN POLYVAGAL TERMS

"Autism in polyvagal terms" refers to a view of autism through the lens of the nervous system and its states of safety, shutdown, and mobilization. The argument rests heavily on the notion that there is a statistically robust and reliable argument to be made that the behaviors we come to know as autism are byproducts of a dysregulated nervous system. Between 1987 and today, what is consistent in findings from over 14 studies done from 1987 to the present on populations of Autists across the lifespan are findings of elevated levels of cardiac activity.

High levels of cardiac activity (i.e., an elevated heart rate) are associated with activation of the sympathetic system, which is responsible for the fight/flight response of the nervous system, and of the dorsal system, which is responsible for the shutdown or collapse response of the nervous system. Because an elevated resting heart rate maintains activation of the sympathetic and/ or dorsal system(s) and prevents activation of the ventral vagal system—which is responsible for things like social engagement, connection, and access to understanding one's feelings—people with consistently elevated levels of cardiac activity will likely struggle with all ventral vagal functions. Thus, any human who is unable to access their ventral state—due to, for example, elevated levels of cardiac activity, such as those found in people diagnosed with autism—is more likely to become increasingly inflexible and rigid and less likely to be able to process social information and engage via biological behaviors like eye contact (Zahn et al., 1987; Van Hecke et al., 2009; Metzler et al., 2013; Porges et al., 2013; Porges et al., 2014; Kushki et al., 2014; Neuhaus et al., 2014; Smeekens et al., 2015; Miller et al., 2017; Bricout et al., 2018; Patriquin et al., 2019; Corbett et al., 2019; Owens et al., 2021; Parma et al., 2021; Goodman, 2016).

One might, then, view the characteristics we come to know as autism (i.e., restrictive, repetitive patterns of interest and behavior and deficits in social engagement) as byproducts of a dysregulated autonomic system. It is important to bear in mind, however, that while there is an increased likelihood of Autists like us living in sympathetic and dorsal states, this is not the only state our nervous systems can and do reside in. Many Autists experience all three nervous system states—ventral, sympathetic, and dorsal—and while, statistically Autists tend to get "stuck" in a sympathetic or dorsal state, we also can and do experience life in our ventral vagal state, where we are better able to co-regulate, engage socially, and integrate emotional experience—capacities supported by the ventral vagal system when cues of safety are effectively detected and internalized. With the work of neural exercises, all people can increase the amount of time we spend in this ventral state.

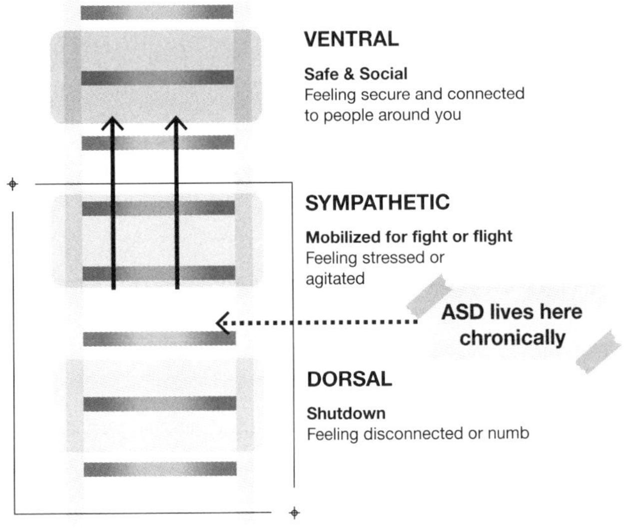

The Autonomic Ladder

Adapted from POLYVAGAL FLIP CHART: UNDERSTANDING THE SCIENCE OF SAFETY by Deb Dana. Copyright © 2020 by Deborah A. Dana. Used by permission of W. W. Norton & Company, Inc.

CONFOUNDING VARIABLES: WHAT ELSE MIGHT BE RAISING YOUR HEART RATE?

Confounding variables are factors that may influence the results of a study and complicate the researchers' ability to answer scientific questions. For example, if a study aimed to observe the effects of melatonin on sleep, but only some participants drank coffee before bed, coffee (caffeine) would be a *confounding variable* in the study's results. As we consider nervous system dysregulation and its correlation to autism, it's important to look for other factors that may be causing one to experience an elevated resting heart rate. Once these factors, if any, are addressed, the disordering aspects of the Autistic experience may improve. To that end, I present here a list of confounding variables that are known to increase heartbeats per minute.

Variables Known to Increase Heartbeats per Minute

1. History of: cyclical vomiting, celiac disease, irritable bowel syndrome, Crohn's disease, or dyspepsia (Kolacz et al., 2023, Kranz et al., 2022, Soares-Miranda et al., 2012)

2. History of acute stress disorders or an anxiety disorder, such as social anxiety, phobias, etc. (Sigrist et al., 2021; Sharma et al., 2011)

3. History or present experience of a protective adoption, or foster home placement (Golfenshtein et al., 2016; Sigrist et al., 2020)

4. Use of any of the following medications: lozaril, xanomeline, oxybutynin, ipratropium bromide, pyridostigmine, atropine, risperidone, Geodon, Abilify, Invega, Fanapt, Latuda, diphenhydramine, or chlorpheniramine, brompheniramine, Terfenadine, hydroxyzine (Saito et al., 2015; Speer et al., 2019; Speer et al., 2021; Wang et al., 2006; Tune,

2001; Gerretsen & Pollock, 2011; Lieberman, 2004; Berdai et al., 2012)

These confounding variables are often used as tools to exclude subjects from studies on heart rate variability, but we can use them to help us understand how our bodies' increased heart rate may increase the likelihood of sympathetic and dorsal activation. For example, autism aside, the use of any of the medications listed above may increase anyone's resting heart rate and thus may increase their chances of experiencing a dysregulated nervous system. If it's possible to decrease, remove, modify, or properly treat any of these variables, you may experience an improvement in your disordering Autist experiences. (If your confounding variables are medical conditions or medications, do not make any changes without consulting your doctor.)

AUTISM AND PROTECTIVE PARTS

Adults with autism can see, through the lens of the autonomic nervous system (ANS), parts that express themselves in the form of "stuckness" and disconnection from the Self. Stuckness itself may take numerous forms, but it might be best illustrated by this example of a patient of mine, who was stuck on why only three people showed up to a writing group he created. Unable to move past this, our session was spent going round and round this one topic. He appeared to be shielding himself from experiencing something. As we sat with the roots of his rumination, what emerged was his concern around honoring the legacy of his deceased lover, as he had started the group as a way to honor the memory of her love of writing. While at the surface he was seemingly stuck on something mundane, beneath the superficial preoccupation with the number of attendees was a much deeper pain. When we look at this example through the lens of the ANS, we see how the Self is a construct of parts like this; in this case, a "fixer" part managed away the pain of loss by repeating the same strategy of ruminating on something less painful.

These expressions are momentary and shift with heart rate. To better understand this point, consider this story about a break-up that was recently told to me during a session with my Autist client Jack. Jack had a romantic partner who called him to tell him that things were off and that she felt unsure about the relationship. She did this over FaceTime, and, naturally, Jack became very cross that she initiated such a vulnerable and difficult conversation over the phone. I observed his body language as he recalled the story during our session: He crossed his arms and slumped over, indicating an increasingly dorsal presentation as the story went on. With his spine giving, inch by inch, I could see the pain in his glassy, unfocused eyes and could feel the ache in his being.

Any fly on the wall listening to Jack could hear the pain in his voice as if almost offering a portal into the moment. "I asked her, 'When did it change for you?'" he said, eyes toward the ground as he sat in the chair across from me. His head looking downward, eyes following his neck, oriented toward the ground, and shoulder sinking, one could clearly see the pain he was in. These signs (eyes staring downward, drooping neck) reflect a body in a state of collapse, a reflection of dorsal activation if you will. A protector who reflects the energy of this very real and salient pain. Relationships, much like humans, are dynamic and changing, and require a certain degree of flexibility. In Autists, what I've observed clinically and in my own experience is that the symptoms we refer to as autism are actually protective strategies. These protective strategies might look like statements guised as questions, emotions like sadness parading as anger, or posture like that of collapsing shoulders. These all reflect a part moving through "fight mode" and into shutdown.

WHEN IS AUTISM DISORDERING?

To understand when autism does and does not fit the definition of a disorder, we must consider the whole field of mental health rather than limiting our discussion solely to developmental disorders, as is traditionally the case for autism and its treatment approaches. By taking a wider view of human psychology and neurophysiology, we will be able, as we did with our definition of Self, to draw on multiple theories to form an interpersonal neurobiological view of autism, as we did with our definition of Self. First, we will define the terms *acute reaction*, *chronic reaction*, and *disorder*; then we will discuss acute versus chronic reactions, describe what constitutes a disorder, and, finally, lay out how neural exercises create an opportunity for those in the neurodivergent community to shift into their ventral vagal state and experience a greater sense of safety.

Term Definitions

1. **Acute Reaction**—a reflection of arousal in the autonomic nervous system that is immediate, severe, sudden, and occurs sporadically.

2. **Chronic Reaction**—a reflection of arousal in the autonomic nervous system that is long-lasting and occurs regularly.

3. **Disorder**—per the *DSM-5*, "a syndrome characterized by clinically significant disturbance in an individual's cognition, emotion regulation, or behavior that reflects a dysfunction in the psychological, biological, or developmental processes underlying mental functioning" (APA, 2013, p. 20).

Acute Versus Chronic Autonomic Arousal

For a pattern of autonomic arousal (the arousal, or activation, of one's nervous system) to be considered a disorder, it must be chronic. For example, the ongoing presence of fear that is disproportionate to the stimuli over a period of time is diagnosed as generalized anxiety disorder. An acute expression of fear, such as a panic attack caused by something that is present and very scary, is a very real experience of fear; but if it is an isolated event, it does not constitute a disorder. Fear itself—a transient energetic experience—is not a disordered reflection of the sympathetic branch of the autonomic nervous system. Only a *chronic* expression of fear across the body, mind, and heart reflects a disorder, such as generalized anxiety disorder.

Much like anxiety, which can manifest as either acute or chronic expressions of fear, autism reflects a real difference that can be experienced acutely or chronically and may indicate the nervous system is locked in a threat response. For example, a once-adaptive state of interest in some aspect of the world can indeed become a strong need for sameness. A popular illustration of this example is represented by the character Sheldon, in the TV show *The Big Bang Theory*, whose Autistic behaviors manifest in his hyperfocused interest (and resultant aptitude) in particle physics as well as in his many rigid needs, such as his inflexible need to be sung the song "Soft Kitty" when he is sick. Thus, while expressions of autism are real and valid reflections of personhood, they can and do become disordered for some people in the neurodiverse community.

Perspectives for Framing Autism

In more widely embraced traditional behaviorist views of autism, wherein autism is seen as a disorder, these very real, acute expressions of narrow interests and the accompanying social differences are perceived as chronic, unchanging, and immutable. Based on this view, the Social Security Administration considers individuals with certain autism diagnoses eligible for lifelong Social Security Insurance benefits; this perspective and diagnosis is also used in schools—it is one of several conditions that qualifies a child for an Individualized Education Plan (IEP). Likewise, features of autism are considered chronic in more identity-based framings of autism. The difference between these two perspectives is that an identity-based understanding of autism calls for the neuromajority to learn to cope with the chronic differences of those with autism, while a disorder-based understanding of autism calls for scaffolded support to help those with autism to assimilate into neurotypical culture *in spite of* their chronic differences. Conversely, the Polyvagal Theory understanding of autism, a third perspective, sees autism as neither a lifelong, immutable disorder nor as an identity but rather as a byproduct of a dysregulated nervous system that can, with practice, become more regulated. A Polyvagal Theory perspective of autism considers members of the autism community to be diverse, including some who are locked into chronic expressions of defense (e.g., emotional blindness or cognitive rigidity) and others who are better able to regulate their nervous systems and, thus, experience less disadvantageous manifestations of their autism. The support offered via Polyvagal Theory provides opportunities to those who experience their nervous systems as locked in chronic states of threat.

By learning to flip the vagal switch via neural exercises (like those outlined in this book), members of the neurodivergent community seeking state changes are afforded a greater number of opportunities for social engagement via a felt sense of safety (neuroception). And so, while not compromising the creativity and unique ways of thinking of those in the neurodivergent community, neural exercises provide a vehicle by which those who feel locked into disordered patterns of autonomic arousal may downshift into states of safety.

A BOTTOM-UP PERSPECTIVE

While the experience of being neurodivergent and Autist can be disordering, as it can interrupt our experience of connection by trapping us in chronic states of sympathetic and dorsal activation, the Autist body holds its own inherent wisdom. Utilizing neural exercises can help unlock this wisdom for the purposes of greater flexibility and connection to others. Thus, this text is written from the perspective that wisdom originates in the human body and informs the mind, rather than from the exclusive view that the brain alone drives human behavior.

Bottom-up wisdom refers to a belief that the self begins in the body, then works its way up to emotions and then thoughts. Throughout this book, we will map Autist experiences of the world (such as stuckness and disconnection) across five domains of experience called *Core Organizers*, a concept that originated in Sensorimotor Psychotherapy. A helpful way to remember these five categories of experience is with the acronym 5 MICE: 5 Sense Perceptions: Movements, Internal Sensations, Cognitions, and Emotions (Ogden & Fisher, 2015). In the coming chapters, I further discuss an experience of rigidity and disconnection from the world.

A key point that I like to share with Autist clients and to remember for myself is that I do think we, the Autistic population, have a propensity to rely on what my colleague Tamilyn White, so eloquently calls "the prison of our minds." Logically speaking, however, if relying on cognition alone actually worked, you wouldn't be here, on this page, trying to find a better, less-disordering way to exist. Western society and thought largely emerged from top-down philosophy: With the emergence of the printing press came the emergence of widespread reading, and the eventual emergence of Martin Luther's 95 theses, the splitting of the Catholic church, and, ultimately, the dawn of the Enlightenment era in Western countries. Autistic people are not exempt from the influence of Western history and, in my clinical opinion, are even more likely than neurotypical folks to engage in top-down methods of thinking. I do not in any way mean to dismiss the contributions of our societies' Cartesian ways of organization, but in contrast to "cogito, ergo sum" (i.e., "I think, therefore I am"), a bottom-up lens that places greater emphasis on the body and its inherent wisdom allows us to unlock our Autist experience by flipping the vagal switch for deeper connection and more flexibility.

PULLING IT ALL TOGETHER

As we have unpacked, the Autist Self uses multiple and consistent adaptive strategies that present as patterns of emoting, thinking, and behaving across time and context. This definition draws on the work of Siegel's concept of the self, Schwartz's parts theory, and Ogden's adaptive strategy theory. Building on these works, we laid out a foundation for the Autist experience of being frequently stuck in sympathetic (fight or flight) and dorsal (shutdown) states of activation—what is likely a chronic state for many unaware Autists. With our understanding of the desirable ventral vagal state, which allows us to connect with others, relax, and understand our emotions, and which is frequently unavailable to many Autists, we can begin to see the opportunities presented by applying neural exercises that will "flip the vagal switch." And while not every Autist experience is disordering, some can be and are disordering, resulting in greater disconnection from others and an increased sense of rigidity. Neural exercises rely on drawing on the wisdom of the body in order to alter our thoughts, emotions, and behaviors.

The following chapters dive into how we can shift away from rigidity and social disengagement and toward greater levels of connection and flexibility. This change is achieved via a series of neural exercises that are presented at the end of each chapter. While Polyvagal Theory remains a theoretical explanation for autism (which can be further explored in my prior work *Autism in Polyvagal Terms*, for those who are interested in taking a deeper dive), these exercises are also rooted in a range of evidence-based approaches including motivational interviewing, clinical social work pedagogy, sensorimotor psychotherapy, mindfulness, biofeedback, and cultivating a felt sense of safety.

3

Empathy and Safety

DO WE LACK EMPATHY?

One particular struggle we Autists may face in our day-to-day interactions is a lack of empathy. People with autism often have a hard time with what Simon Baron-Cohen called *theory of mind*, which refers to a person's ability to conceptualize the thoughts, motives, feelings, and experiences of others (Baron-Cohen, 1991). People with autism tend to lack this ability, which can lead to difficulties relating with others. It is important to note that Baron-Cohen argues that this is not the result of a deficit in character (no one is accusing Autists of being "bad" people); rather, it is entirely a deficit in ability. This chapter explores the biobehavioral relationship between increased cardiac activity and its impact on what we have come to know as empathy.

Recapping the topics in Chapters 1 and 2, the vagus nerve has three branches, known as the dorsal, sympathetic, and ventral vagal systems, and studies have found Autists to consistently have higher heart rates than neurotypical people, which increases the likelihood that they will be in a sympathetic (i.e., fight-or-flight) state. If one's nervous system is under enough stress, the dorsal system will become activated. The dorsal system is the most primitive of the three systems and is often linked to what are known as shutdown responses (Dana, 2021). These shutdown responses are primitive, linked to surviving among predators; our reptilian ancestors gave us the evolutionary survival strategies of freeze, fold, faint, feign death, and disassociate. Responsible for immobilizing the body in a last-ditch attempt to escape danger, the dorsal response also shuts down our social engagement systems in its attempt to increase our chances of survival.

What happens when this cranial nerve's ability to control things like head turning, vocalizing, controlling one's jaw, attuning one's middle ear muscles, orienting one's eyes, and moving one's neck (Porges, 2023) become interrupted by these ancient survival strategies? All of these autonomic nervous system functions go offline when this ancient survival pattern emerges due to activation of the dorsal system. To put it more plainly, if my body is stuck in a dorsal state and is thus unable to orient to someone speaking by making eye contact and attuning my ears, how on Earth could I be able to even begin to conceptualize what others might be thinking and feeling or what their motivations and experiences might be?

Considering a lack of empathy from the perspective of an overactive dorsal vagal system takes the conversation from "lack of ability" to considering a nervous system that is constantly in survival mode. While the evidence of the relationship between theory of mind and dorsal system activation is still preliminary, a meta-analysis (a study of studies) that examined six studies of typically developing people yielded a significant relationship between lack of empathy and high dorsal activation (Zammuto et al., 2021). The central argument here is that the Autistic mind is directly influenced by the Autistic body, which may often be physically unable to orient itself to other people due to the fear response triggered by dorsal vagal system activation, which the body of the individual with autism may be "locked into" due to frequent dorsal activation.

THE AUTIST MIND FOLLOWS THE BODY

Succinctly put, Autists can and do at times lack empathy. As outlined earlier, the Autist mind follows the body, which, from current cardiac evidence, along with more neurochemical and evolutionary lines of thought—appears to be a body hijacked by its own dorsal and sympathetic systems. In this sense, a lack of empathy in an Autist is not a defect of the Autist's character but, rather, the result of a fast-moving internal world that is disconnected from its own internal emotions and physical sensations. When I write *sensations*, I'm referring to our body's signals about its emotional and physical needs (Sensorimotor

Psychotherapy Institute, 2023); by *emotions*, I am referring to the energetic responses to the body that are often indicative of relational patterns and that shape behavioral responses to situations at multiple levels of consciousness.

The internal experience of this inability to orient to the present is known as dissociation. The term *dissociation* refers to "experiencing a loss of connection between thoughts, memories, feelings, surroundings, behaviors, and identity" (Mayo Clinic, 2023). According to Pierre Janet, one of the earliest theorists on the subject, dissociation is "a disrupted . . . integration of psychological functions and an altered state of consciousness" (as cited in van der Kolk & van der Hart, 1989). The process of dissociation is mediated by the dorsal vagus branch of the autonomic nervous system. Consider the following example, from one of my clients, which illustrates how disconnection from one's own emotions due to loss of autonomic function might impact relationships.

I was familiar with my Autist client Kelsey's close friend George, because during our sessions, Kelsey spoke often of George as a source of support and friendship. George had held space for Kelsey during some of her deepest moments of pain and was what Kelsey called her "ride or die" friend. However, one day Kelsey came to a session looking visibly agitated. She told me that the night before, while on the phone with George, she had told him, "If you just looked different I would totally date you, and probably would have made you my boyfriend some time ago." Understandably upset, George replied, "I know you are in pain, but this is not okay. I can't be your friend anymore.

Please don't call me." To this day, George still does not want to be friends with Kelsey. And frankly, who can blame him?

In this story, with George and Kelsey, we see that Kelsey was unable to anticipate what George's response might be to her statement, which then caused a rupture in the relationship. To fully understand this interaction, it's crucial to know the context of their conversation. Several months earlier, Kelsey's fiancé Josh had unexpectedly left her. This loss affected her deeply, so much so that during our sessions she regularly reported that her body felt full of pain. These chronic pain signals likely elicited a fair amount of dorsal system activation. In fact, I had often noted that when Kelsey discussed her former fiancé during our sessions, she exhibited signs of dissociation: depersonalization, derealization, issues with memory, confusion in identity, emotional numbing, and an altered perception of time. Before telling George that she would have dated him if he looked different, they had been discussing the fact that Kelsey had seen a post on social media showing Josh with a new girlfriend. Kelsey was, understandably, in a lot of pain, and likely in a state of dorsal shutdown. Unable to access even her own emotions, she did not have the capacity in that moment to anticipate the effect her words would have on her friend.

In this full account of the situation, we can imagine how Kelsey's dorsal system may have won out in her interaction with George, creating an apparent lack of empathy—but it's a lack of empathy that is contextually dependent and relevant. More specifically, we see her lack of ability to anticipate the plethora of responses to her statement that would be affected by things like: what George might think about being told that Kelsey would feel differently about him if he "only looked different"; how he might feel being told he isn't good enough for her; what might be motivating him to try to comfort her as a friend; and what experiences and beliefs he may already have had regarding his body. While Kelsey's intentions were not malicious, the hurt that she caused was very real, as was the rupture in this relationship with a dear friend. If this is the type of experience that brings you here, I expect you are seeking answers for how to become aware of when you are lacking this ability and how to flip your vagal switch as needed.

CULTIVATING EMPATHY THROUGH SAFETY

One of the things that repeatedly happens during dorsal and sympathetic activation in acute (not excluding chronic) cases is a decreased level of what is called *executive functioning* (Jonsdottir et al., 2006; Liang et al., 2022; Shields et al., 2016). Executive functioning is the ability to sustain attention on one interest, often in the context of competing interests (Barkley, 2012). According to Barkley, executive functioning is comprised of five areas of behavior: time management, emotional regulation, self-regulation, organization, and motivation. The Autistic experience of lacking empathy is directly related to the inability to sustain the attention necessary to anticipate another person's experience (aan het Rot et al., 2014; Quinde-Zlibut et al., 2021; Li et al., 2023) and, according to the research of Rot et al. (2014), Quinde-Zlibut et al. (2021), and Li et al. (2023), being in a threat state disrupts one's ability to attend to one or more stimuli, such as facial expressions, tone of voice, and intensity of vocal expressions.

To illustrate this, let's consider the example of an Autist child playing tag with her classmates on a playground. After a while, her peers become tired of the game and move on to another activity, but the Autist child continues to tag her friends, who become increasingly annoyed by her tagging them and shouting, "You're it!" The Autist child, perhaps stressed by the environment of the school and the playground, is unable to attend to the stimuli that might clue her in to her friends' displeasure, such as their disgruntled facial expressions or the tone of their voices when they say, "Knock it off!" Her decreased executive functioning, due to dorsal and/or sympathetic activation, prevents her from focusing her attention on her friends' expressions, while a chronic state of threat in her autonomic nervous system may actually physically preclude her from attending to these stimuli. That is, if this young girl is in a chronic dorsal state, she may be neurologically unable to orient her visual attention toward the nonverbal social cues of the other children on the playground (Franchini et al., 2017; Nyström et al., 2019; Billeci et al., 2017; Neuhaus et al., 2014; Patriquin et al., 2019; Guy et al., 2014).

Further, if she fails to reach her desired outcome of getting her friends to rejoin the game, her tags may become more and more forceful. Eventually, one of her peers may, from the force of her tag, fall down, begin to cry, and accuse the Autistic child of pushing her. This would be an example of a relationship ruptured due to the child's inability to anticipate her peers' experiences, much as Kelsey's fifteen-year friendship with George was ruptured by her inability to anticipate his reaction to being told that she would date him if he looked different.

In the experiences of people with autism, lack of empathy in the Autist experience seems to be more survival oriented than intentionally cold and malicious. Because we Autists are often locked in a chronic state of sympathetic or dorsal activation—fluctuating between fight or flight and shutdown modes as our nervous system attempts to protect us from threat—we are often unable to process stimuli that might clue us in to the experiences of others and/or to sustain our attention long enough to anticipate others' experiences. If this is your experience or belief about your own Self, my hope is that you can begin to access a greater and deeper sense of compassion for yourself, for it is only in doing so that you will encounter yourself in a new way. The central task, then, is to facilitate access to one's ventral vagal system, where we experience a sense of safety. Being able to easily access the ventral vagal state is known as vagal efficiency, and this ability can be developed through neural exercises.

NEURAL EXERCISES FOR FLIPPING THE VAGAL SWITCH

In the next section of this chapter, and in all subsequent chapters of this book, you will find an exercise to help you consolidate and apply your learning. Neural exercises are designed to be practiced, and therefore they should be repeated for best results.

While they will have no adverse effects, your Autist experience is unlikely to improve without regular practice. Thus, much like anything we wish to become skilled at, we must put in time and effort. In the Mindful Self-Compassion exercise, Question 5 is designed to be utilized over a span of time. Complete Questions 1 through 4 and take some time to reflect. When you complete the final question, allow it to be a tool you use over time; a mantra, if you will. This can be a gentle reminder of the parts of your experience that you can be grateful for.

Neural Exercise 1:
Mindful Self-Compassion

In this exercise, you are invited to explore your capacity for mindfulness. *Mindfulness* is an ancient strategy that invites users to dwell in the present and to notice their internal state without judgment. At this time, you may have only a limited capacity for mindfulness, and that's okay—many of us live in a constant state of holding the gun of judgment to our head. To the best of your ability, I invite you now to be with this judgment and try to create some internal distance from it. Future chapters and neural exercises will help you gain a greater ability to do this, and you can return to this exercise later and practice again.

1. Think back to a time when you really lacked understanding of another person's experience. This should be a time when your lack of understanding had a direct relational consequence that continues

to cause you some degree of pain. Describe it below. If you can, map out the conversation or situation as it unfolded (all of it, not just the easy parts or your analysis of it).

2. Thinking back on this memory, sense into the most painful part. Pick the words from your description above that trigger the most pain, and write them below.

3. Read the words from Question 2. As you do, what do you notice unfolding in your body? Just be with what unfolds, and describe only the sensations you are experiencing now below.

4. As you really feel into this painful moment, what emotions do you come up against? Do not focus on thoughts (words describing what happened). An *emotion* is an energetic response from the body that may indicate relational patterns and that often shapes our responses to situations at multiple levels of consciousness. When describing your *emotions* below, try to limit your description to emotion words, such as happy, sad, angry, glad, disgusted, mad, joyful, fearful, anxious.

5. As you sit in the muck and the mire of your own mistake, remember that you are not your choices and that your actions may be a byproduct of an Autistic body that sometimes becomes hijacked by your dorsal vagal system. Bearing that in mind, what is one kind thing you might offer to yourself, knowing how little of your capacity for

empathy might be within your conscious control? (For example, "While sometimes what I say really comes off wrong, that doesn't make me a bad person. It does, however, make me a human," or "I often miss other people's feelings, but this doesn't make me a hopeless cause. It means I need to grow and expand a bit.")

Write your kind statement to yourself below, and offer it to yourself as a reminder throughout the week.

Neural Exercise 2:
Noticing the Nothingness

Dissociation is an all-too-common phenomenon and is perhaps understudied in Autist populations. That stated, this exercise is designed to help you begin tracking your own dissociative experiences. Think back to a time when you noticed yourself feeling numb or flat. Someone else may have commented on your lack of expression; perhaps this dissociative experience even caused some relational difficulties. As you sink into this memory, let's use some of the skills from Neural Exercise 1, and work through this memory with self-compassion.

1. As you recall your experience of dissociation, can you remember where your thoughts went in that moment?

2. As you consider this memory, what does it feel like to feel nothing? Any words or descriptors are okay, but begin to bring some awareness to this experience so that it becomes easier to recognize the next time it happens.

3. What do you notice happening in your body as you recall those feelings and thoughts? Is your body tightening, loosening, feeling pain, or something else?

4. As you spend time remembering this experience, what words or phrases come to mind that connect to this space? As you notice them, write them

down—don't overthink it (this might not be easy to do); just list them. These words can serve as a name for this nothingness space and as an anchor to this experience.

4

Masking and Loneliness

> People think that I snap into this character who's really awkward, but it's like, no, I was already really awkward. And I feel like growing up . . . I always just thought I was annoying to people. I feel like they're not wrong, so that's where my insecurities come in. Oh, I am annoying . . .
>
> —**BOBBI ALTHOFF,** *TIKTOK*

Part of what draws listeners to Bobbi Althoff's podcast is her clear disinterest in others' opinions of her—and more specifically, her disinterest in the opinions of her celebrity guests. By interviewing the likes of Drake, Lil Yachty, and other celebrities, Althoff has made a career out of her awkwardness and irreverence. While it may be the case that her awkwardness has led Althoff to great success, she often makes it clear—as she does in this chapter's epigraph—that for her, this is anything but an act. Being awkward is her true Self. And while Althoff has not, to my knowledge, been diagnosed with autism spectrum disorder (ASD), her statement encapsulates a common experience for many Autists: a yearning to be accepted. But acceptance is a fickle thing when it isn't for who one really is. By trying to act acceptable or "cool," we cut ourselves off from the one person we are an expert on: ourselves.

I will refer to this process of alienation of who we Autists are from Self as *masking*. In his popular book *Unmasking Autism*, Devon Price defines masking as "a coping skill for Autistic people to deal with society." In this text, masking will refer to any part of the Self that functions to shield the Self from shame through creative attempts to blend in with or match one's social context. This definition is a bit narrower than Price's definition due to the fact that we define the Self as something that is multiple in nature. Author of *To Be Loved*, Frank Anderson, describes the Self as something everyone has: "Our core, our essence, our internal compass that possesses inherent wisdom and healing capacity" (Anderson, n.d.). From the vantage point of organicity (the internal wisdom of our bodies), the Self is capable of moving toward homeostasis using its own inherent strength. As discussed in prior chapters, the Self is not singular in nature but comprised of parts, some of which are protective while others are exiles (our vulnerable "inner children"). Each part serves a unique function but can be related to via our adult Self.

Our adult Self is the place from which we are most fully ourselves. From a polyvagal perspective, we can consider the adult

Self in terms of our ventral vagal state, the Self from which flexibility, connection, and creativity can emerge. Our adult Self is present in the ventral vagal state and allows us to connect to ourself and to others.

Masking, on the other hand, comes from a part of the Self that is responsible for protecting us from the pain of experiencing ourselves through the eyes of others. Protectors, a type of masking part, execute an adaptive strategy. As discussed earlier, in the original context of Pat Ogden's work, an *adaptive strategy* "is an ecological approach that addresses the relationship of a person with their surroundings" (Sensorimotor Psychotherapy Institute, 2023). From an ANE view of autism, though, *adaptive strategy* is a term used to describe the function of a part in its orientation to survival (e.g., a person learning to become detached from feelings and to not voice their needs because when they were a child they were accused of lying). *Survival* means how an organism orients itself in a specific moment toward what its nervous system perceives as homeostasis. It is important to note, however, that every nervous system has a different version of homeostasis—for example, someone whose nervous system is in a chronic state of sympathetic activation will experience homeostasis differently than someone who is frequently in a ventral state of safety.

Masking can take many forms. Consider the following example from my own experience. One day in the office, I ate some of my coworker's cheese puffs without asking her permission. When she later asked me about it, I said, "Oh, I'm sorry, I was just super hungry and wasn't even thinking." I offered this excuse as much to myself as to my coworker, as a means of experiencing myself in a more positive light and in hopes that I might be accepted by others. While it is possible that I was hungry and that I wasn't thinking about my actions, my explanation did little to nothing to meet my coworker's experience of me not asking before taking her cheese puffs nor to acknowledge the discomfort I caused her.

While this wasn't a big deal, it reflects a time in which I withdrew, both internally (from myself) and externally (from others), and retreated from an opportunity to be vulnerable. If I were being honest with myself and my coworker, I might have said, "Oftentimes I really don't think before I act or speak; it's a bit of a struggle for me. And so it's not that I don't care about how my actions affect you, but I see that is what I communicated to you. I'm really embarrassed about what I did, and I'm hoping I can rebuild your trust in me." This would have allowed me to both communicate my feelings and move toward repairing the rupture in our relationship. In my attempt to shield myself from the pain of the embarrassment that I might have felt from acknowledging what I had done (an adaptive strategy), I actually created a deeper disconnection, both from myself and from my coworker.

This example from my own life illustrates a struggle all people with ASD face as Autists: loneliness. Though it may manifest in subtle ways, such as in my interaction with my coworker, the cumulative effect of years of masking results for many Autists in a deeply agonizing and chronic sense of loneliness. Again, I find that the best way to illustrate this is by sharing my own experience. I have autism; I am an Autist in my mid-thirties; I'm a single father to two boys; I've been divorced for over a decade and live in the middle of nowhere. This comes with a tapestry of lack that provides me with very few opportunities for meeting a partner with whom I can share depth and meaning. Yet, whenever I do happen to meet someone who seems like she could be a potential partner, I get a bit squirrely looking across the plane of possibility. I might make eye contact and not say anything, awkwardly smile, and then beat myself up for days to come due to the shutdown I experienced. I find myself unable to meet that deep desire I have for connection and being known because my dorsal vagal system acts out and the only thing I can muster is a funny-looking glare, which I assume nobody in their right mind can interpret as anything other than creepy. I share this story because it conveys the deep pain I experience at being unable to meet the need, both my own and my boys', of finding someone who is excited about me and who checks off some of my boxes. This pain comes from the fact that even at 35 years old, doctorally educated, published, marathon-finishing, and world-traveling, I often can't muster a simple "hello."

I share this also to demonstrate how loneliness is endemic even in people who may appear to have things figured out. One study, conducted during the COVID-19 pandemic on a group of forty 11- to 16-year-old Autist youths, observed the effects of a single session intervention (SSI) on loneliness (Gerber et al., 2024). The study found that those who received the SSI experienced a decrease in loneliness symptoms, including decreased depressive symptoms associated with loneliness, compared to those in the control group, who did not receive the SSI.

I find loneliness to be a pervasive problem for both myself and my Autist clients, and I believe it to be due in part to the protective masking of parts of ourselves. So, if you too are struggling with loneliness, I invite you to consider the role your dorsal vagal system may be playing in your experiences of disconnection.

DORSAL VAGAL SYSTEM: A SURVIVAL SYSTEM

As covered in Chapter 2, the dorsal vagal system is the oldest branch of the nervous system, and its function is primarily behaviors and anatomical structures that enable the freeze survival response. Located on the medulla oblongata portion of the brain stem, this part of the nervous system is known to induce behaviors and emotions like collapsing, helplessness, hopelessness, numbing, freezing, loss of control of facial and eye muscles, and a reduced heart rate. Originally responsible for functions like freezing (e.g., a deer in headlights), feigning death (e.g., an opossum playing dead or a turtle going into its shell), or fawning (e.g., people pleasing; Bialik, 2024), the dorsal system activates disconnection, making things like eye contact difficult.

Do you remember our example of the Autist child playing tag on the playground? Eventually the other children don't want to play tag anymore, but this one child continues to tag them because tagging is fun, and because she isn't able to process the social information that indicates to other children that the game is over. This is likely a child who is "stuck" in her dorsal vagal system, who is physically unable to attune to her surroundings and understand that her peers are no longer interested in being tagged. Similarly, when I took my coworker's cheese puffs without asking, my nervous system was also likely in a dorsal state, inhibiting me from processing the social information necessary to anticipate how my coworker might feel about this. And so, behaviors tagging someone against their will or taking their cheese puffs without their consent might be the result of being caught in an overactive dorsal vagal system.

As an Autist, not being able to process social information, like whether or not someone wants to play or share with us, becomes a pretty deep barrier to connection. I would contend that the experience is a bit like being on autopilot rather than having an engaged prefrontal cortex or fully online adult Self. The masking part takes over to protect us from the consequences of our own shame. Again, masking is a reflection of dorsal vagal activation and refers to any part of the Self that functions to shield the Self from shame by creative attempts to blend in with or match one's social context. While this attempt at being "cool" or fitting in is meant to help us survive (think back to when being accepted by one's tribe was literally essential to human survival), it is likely to lead us to disconnect from ourselves and from the very essence of who we are. Being vulnerable becomes an immeasurably difficult task when operating from a place of disconnection; and if one functions from this place of disconnection for long enough, the behavior can become patterned, meaning the autonomic nervous system (ANS) can develop a propensity for holding specific states over periods of time as an unconscious reaction to a perceived threat, which may or may not be there. Neural exercises can help us shift out of these chronic states of threat.

LOVE ON THE SPECTRUM

The popular Netflix series *Love on the Spectrum* introduced many viewers to the challenges people with ASD face in a romantic relationship. Romantic relationships, indeed, seem to be where most Autist ASD clients of mine tend to show up least authentically.

At 28 years old, Jeff's romantic history was a bit of a wild jungle of stories. Despite his many good qualities, including his sincerity and generally laid-back nature, his struggle to predict his partners' experiences of his words and actions had ruptured many relationships over the years. Jill, unlike the vast majority of his partners, was someone he had been able to make it work with. However, one day he came to our session with dark circles beneath his eyes and admitted that he and Jill had been arguing the night before. They had been at a bar with two of Jill's friends. Whenever they spent time with these two friends, Jeff tended not to say much, preferring to observe the interactions between Jill and her friends. When her friends asked if Jeff and Jill wanted to dance, Jeff declined, and Jill stayed with him at the bar while her friends went out onto the dance floor. Jill looked at Jeff for a moment and took a long drink. Then she asked him, "Why don't you like my friends?"

Jeff laughed at the question, and Jill became visibly upset. Unphased, Jeff replied honestly, "Because they treat you like shit." Jill sneered at this, and, during our session, Jeff admitted to me that he wasn't sure how to interpret her expression. He was feeling detached from any kind of emotion, and the dark, loud space of the bar was starting to feel surreal. When Jill said nothing, he pressed on.

"Look," he told her, "you give them so much and I, for the life of me, can't understand what it is they give you back. You are the last person they call, they give you maybes, and they struggle to plan with you. Why would I like them?"

Like many of Jeff's comments, this feedback demonstrated a lack of connection to a ventral space of the adult Self. If Jeff had been in his adult Self, he might have been able to pause and respond in a way that more clearly fit the moment. For instance, instead of fighting when Jill said, "Why don't you like my friends?", he might have noticed Jill's expressions of fear of danger (e.g., the shortness of her question, her withdrawal from the larger group). A more regulated response that tapped into his adult Self might have sounded like, "I hear the pain in your question. What am I missing here?"

But things didn't go that way; instead, too late, he noticed that tears were collecting in her eyes. She replied, "Jeff, they're my family. How do you not get this?" She quickly left the bar, and Jeff trailed after her, struggling to keep up with her brisk pace and realizing that there was something he wasn't getting.

Despite how right Jeff might have been about how Jill's friends treated her, in that moment, there were key cues from Jill's nervous system that Jeff wasn't receiving. His level of stress or how tired he was may have contributed to an elevated heart rate, which in turn may have increased his rigidity (i.e., continuing to insist that Jill's friends treated her poorly despite Jill's cues that he was upsetting her). If Jeff had been able to slow down, access his adult Self, and consider these cues, it may have changed his relational outcome with Jill.

NEURAL EXERCISES FOR FLIPPING THE VAGAL SWITCH

As discussed in Chapter 2, organicity and openness are guiding values that drive the change created by neural exercises, which are intended to facilitate a sense of safety. To reiterate, *organicity* refers to "the internal wisdom of all living systems. Thus a therapist does not 'heal' the client; rather the healing power and intelligence is within each person who has their own unique, mysterious, and emergent growth path" (Sensorimotor Psychotherapy Institute, 2023). Neural exercises can help unlock Autists' inherent bodily wisdom to ease social experiences and hence decrease loneliness.

Openness refers to "the ability to shift from existing perspectives to move into new and underexplored ways of thinking" (Sensorimotor Psychotherapy Institute, 2023). If this value had been in play the evening Jeff was at the bar with Jill and her friends, there may have been a different ending to their story. His rigid "Look" might have come out as, "What I notice when . . ." The latter possesses a different spirit altogether, one that encapsulates the regulation needed to be open to the possibility that one's perceptions or judgments are wrong, or at least not helpful. Thus, I invite you to consider what possibilities might become accessible to you through the regular practice of neural exercises like those presented in this book. Might there be instances, such as this moment between Jeff and Jill, in your life where a greater degree of flexibility could strengthen your relationships and decrease your loneliness?

Neural Exercise 3:
The Biofeedback Plan

Biofeedback is a type of therapy that can help clients learn to control certain bodily functions—such as breathing, heart rate, and muscle tension—for the purpose of improving both physical and mental well-being. In the context of this book, I use the term *biofeedback* to refer to a set of physical activities, performed over a set duration and period of time, for the purpose of developing more flexible thinking and behavioral patterns. Physical exercise is known to shift the time between heartbeats, moving the nervous system out of a sympathetic state and into a ventral state. This shift increases mental flexibility, which in turn decreases one's sense of being "stuck" and increases one's ability to be open to new experiences. By noticing the effects of physical activity on your thinking and behavioral patterns, you can use your observations to learn to control some symptoms of rigidity and social disengagement using physical exercise. It can be argued that there are more or less effective ways of engaging in exercise, and the science of kinesiology likely has things to say on this, but for the purpose of practicing biofeedback in order to be more open and flexible in the way you exist in the world, I invite you to not worry about all that. Rather, the point of this neural exercise is to experiment with exercising regularly so that you can determine what frequency and types of exercise allow you to experience an improvement in your cognitive and behavioral flexibility. To that end, I share below a biofeedback plan I created in 2023, including my target goal, a record of how I implemented the plan, and some of the relational outcomes I experienced. Following my example is a section for you, the reader, to develop and fill in your own biofeedback plan and track your use of this neural exercise. I have also included questions to guide you as you notice changes in flexibility.

I want to make it clear that in no way should my own sample biofeedback plan be considered a standard for others to hold themselves against. Comparing yourself to my 2023 plan would be to miss the point of organicity entirely. A biofeedback plan needs to be created in the context of your own Autistic bodily wisdom. If you so choose, pairing your own bodily wisdom with the guidance of athletic trainers and/or physicians may provide even better results, though the exercise can also be practiced on your own.

2023 Biofeedback Plan Example

Target Flexibility Goal: Greater emotional flexibility in romantic relationships (i.e., I'll be better able to handle ambiguity from partners)

Implementation Period: May 2023–September 2023

Biofeedback Interventions: (1) Hot yoga at a yoga studio in Chippewa Falls, WI, including classes like 26:2, Sculpt, and C-Yoga with inversions. (2) Run 2–3 miles each day of the week, for a total of 14 miles per week.

Frequency:

(1) Hot Yoga (days I went to class):

June 1, 3, 4, 6, 10, 12, 13, 14, 17, 19, 20, 23, 24, 26, 27, 30; July 1, 2, 4, 5, 6, 8, 11, 16, 18, 21, 22, 23, 16; August 1, 2, 5, 6, 7, 8, 9, 10, 11, 13, 15, 17, 21, 25, 30; September 3, 4, 6, 7, 8, 9, 10, 12, 14, 16, 17, 18, 25

(2) Running (miles run per week):

June: Week 1: 12 miles, Week 2: 14 miles, Week 3: 18 miles, Week 4: 14 miles; July: Week 1: 10 miles, Week 2: 9 miles, Week 3: 5 miles, Week 4: 14 miles; August: Week 1: 15 miles, Week 2: 13 miles, Week 3: 12 miles, Week 4: 14 miles; September: Week 1: 10 miles, Week 2: 4 miles, Week 3: 5 miles, Week 4: 3 miles

Observations: June: I met no new women this month who really are in my age range, but I was, in fact, able to process with grace my oldest son's anger about not getting to watch something on the iPad. This was new.

July: I made three female friends this month (two new, one returning) and got invited to go to a bar. I froze up when the woman invited me to the bar and couldn't really make a move. Perhaps it's old trauma, but I got really stuck on some dumb detail.

August: I ended up going on one date, and I hung out once with the same woman as I did in July. In both instances I froze up again. I think the woman from July might be into me, but it's hard to be flexible enough to think I'm attractive enough for her. I don't really see myself that way.

September: Things ended with the woman from August because I told her I missed her too soon. That was rough. On the other hand, I had a little more compassion for myself and managed to land in a situationship with the woman from July and August. This is new, and I appear to be able to move through the freeze phase a bit easier, and I know I have been more flexible because she changes plans a lot. As I found a happy balance between yoga and running, I noticed an increased ability to tolerate the ambiguity and uncertainty of the situationship, whereas when I missed weeks with each exercise, I lost the ability to tolerate the uncertainty.

Notes on Openness and Organicity From This Example: Organicity is an attitude we can have toward ourselves as well as toward others. It means being open to the possibility that some of the time you might not hit your goals, and it invites us to be open with ourselves. For instance, if you look at my running frequency, it takes a real nosedive in July and September because in July I took a vacation to Pennsylvania to see one of my favorite authors speak, and in September I went back to teaching child psychology at a local university. My purpose in sharing this is to illustrate how organicity is something we must embody if we desire to increase our sense of openness and flexibility around our goals, like increased emotional intimacy. Practicing organicity leads to the need to be open, and this in turn increased my flexibility toward romantic partners.

My Biofeedback Plan

Target Flexibility Goal:

Implementation Period or Initiation Date:

Biofeedback Interventions:

Intervention 1:

Intervention 2:

Frequency:

Observations:

Neural Exercise 4:
Mindful Word Counting

Mindfulness refers to the process of being in the present moment, noticing when one's attention drifts from the moment, and gently resuming attention to the present moment. One thing I've noticed about myself and those I work with is that we tend to live with a great deal of judgment toward ourselves and others. When working with clients, I often use the following exercise to introduce them to the experience of mindfulness. I now invite you, too, to experience the power of mindfulness, which I suspect will grow on you with time. This neural exercise is one you will want to repeat—mindfulness is a skill that takes practice because it is in the practice of noticing without judgment that we grow and we begin to realize how very frequently we judge things.

Mindfulness Exercise

Pick a period of time, such as an afternoon or an evening, and count the number of times you say the words "the" and "and." Try to notice this with gentle curiosity rather than judgment. The point of this exercise is not to analyze your use of these words; the point is to simply stay rooted in the present moment by noticing something mundane, such as your use of these common words. Because there is no inherent value associated with your use of an everyday word such as "the" or "and" (it's neither "bad" nor "good" to use these words), this is an effective way to practice noticing without judgment.

1. How many times did you notice yourself saying "the"? "And"?

2. How did it feel to mindfully notice your use of these words without judgment?

A PARTING THOUGHT

While at face value, an exercise like observing the number of times one says "the" and "and" may seem simple, my hunch is that if your brain is anything like mine, you found this exercise difficult. Judging is so automatic and second nature to us that it takes work to not function from a place of judgment. Don't beat yourself up if you found yourself judging or analyzing rather than staying mindfully present. To embody mindfulness, the most important thing is to begin with an attitude of nonjudgment, and then to practice noticing when we are judging and gently bring ourselves back to the present moment.

5

Accessing Our Emotions

ALEXITHYMIA AND AUTISM

Alexithymia is, for our purposes, a difficulty with describing and labeling one's feelings. Originally born from research in the field of psychoanalysis and one of the more enduring Freudian constructs that remains today in the field of psychology, this concept is hyper-present in populations like those with autism and posttraumatic stress disorder. A meta-analysis performed by Kinnaird et al. (2019) looked at a variety of samples of Autistic adults and determined that around 50% of Autistic adults meet the criteria for alexithymia.

Alexithymia can be a personality trait that manifests as an adaptive way of being detached from oneself—in other words, it's a form of masking. Alexithymia may serve the purpose of shielding people from the distress of their emotions, but it can also prevent them from experiencing a rich inner life and can lead to behavior that hurts others. For example, one Christmas day I sent a very hurtful email to an ex who had broken up with me eight months earlier. Because I wasn't able to process my own intense emotions around this breakup, I was dysregulated and cut off from any sense of empathy toward my ex. I was not able to anticipate the harm I might cause her by sending an email that touched on some of her deepest insecurities. Thus, alexithymia can result in not only a deep disconnection from ourselves, but also in behavior that prevents connection with others.

This personality construction forms in the context of these two elements: high levels of cardiac activity—which trigger chronic sympathetic or dorsal activation (our threat states) and block access to the ventral vagal state, where a sense of connection to oneself and others is possible—and an underlying assumption of *mistrust*. What can help to alleviate alexithymia, then, is enhancing one's felt sense of safety. A *felt sense of safety* is a preconscious way in which our bodies know ease based on conditions in our social environment. Certain conditions bring us into ventral vagal state (enhancing our felt sense of safety), while other conditions take us out of ventral vagal state; all of this can happen outside of our conscious awareness.

CULTIVATING A FELT SENSE OF SAFETY IN ORDER TO ACCESS EMOTIONS

In this neural exercise, based in Sensorimotor Psychotherapy (SP), I introduce you to a method of accessing your feelings in a deeper way. SP can help us experience feelings in a non-threatening way because it allows us to first experience them through the body's nonverbal sensory cues. SP-based neural exercises are intended to widen one's felt sense of flexibility and to increase one's openness to relationships via the regulating power of the body.

I offer the caveat that this neural exercise may not be for everyone. For some Autists, the body can be a very dysregulating place, especially if it is storing traumatic memories, such as those of being sexually or physically assaulted. If you have experienced this kind of trauma, I encourage you to proceed with this exercise *with caution* and perhaps seek the help of a professional. This neural exercise also will not be of any benefit to people who have never experienced a safe place (a space in which you feel at ease and are able to internally and externally let your guard down), because it asks that you enter an imagined or remembered safe place in your mind.

I invite you to approach this neural exercise with two of our values in mind: *respect* and *kindness*. To reiterate, *kindness* is responding in the gentlest and easiest way we can, achieved by being attuned to our own autonomic nervous system and the nervous systems of others (Inderbitzen, 2024). *Respect* is valuing individual and professional diversity, demonstrating intentionality, kindness, communication, and egalitarianism (MINT, n.d.). We approach Neural Exercise 5 with this sense of ease via respect and kindness in order to enhance our felt sense of safety. In this way, we may begin to remove our masks and better access our own feelings, which in turn can, in the context of safe social connectedness, relieve our loneliness.

Neural Exercise 5:
Cultivating a Felt Sense of Safety

I invite you to close your eyes for a moment, and as you do, picture a place where you feel safe. Give it a minute, don't rush it, and just really be in it. Now, pick a sense. For this example, let's use touch.

In this safe space, notice what an imagined surface might feel like against your hand. Is it rough? Is it soft?

Now, easing back into your safe place, sense into your feet. What do you notice? Are they on a solid, supportive surface or on something more yielding, like a pillow?

Now sense even further into the sensations of your feet. What do you notice about the texture? The temperature?

Do you notice any emotions that accompany these sensations? If the feeling word or phrase that comes to mind is something that would only make sense to you, that's okay. It may be tempting to try to describe your feelings using conventional terms like "happy" or "calm," but the point of this exercise is to get in touch with your particular unique felt sense of safety, which may be better described as "floating" or "like sunshine" (just to name a couple examples).

Observations

What I and many of my Autistic clients find difficult about this exercise is the temptation to describe rather than experience an emotion. Returning to the example of the email I sent to an ex, I was unable at that time to be with my feelings of pain, and rather than just being with my own pain energetically, I communicated that pain to my ex in a ruthless way that struck at her insecurities. If I had been able to fully feel and process my pain, I might have been able to communicate productively with my ex, from a safe and resourced place. The body can be a naturally resourceful force within the human experience, and so my expectation and hope is that this exercise may have given you some sense of ease or harmony in your life. This neural exercise, like the others presented in the book, is meant to be integrated into your life as an ongoing practice rather than as a one-time intervention. It takes effort and practice to sense into your body and notice its sensations and, from there, your emotions. As I often teach other therapists, emotions might be something some Autists can experience only cognitively at first. And if this is true for you, as it was for me, it's okay if this neural exercise takes some repetition and practice. Again, the invitation is to maintain a spirit of *kindness* and *respect* toward yourself. Learning to slow down a nervous system that has many years of experience living in a chronic state of threat will likely take some time.

We might also think of this exercise as a process of unlearning, as your nervous system is *un*learning its chronic activation. Unlearning is a natural process of adulthood, so if you are highly critical of yourself, like I am of myself, and have a difficult time accepting yourself as you are, I'd like to share with you an invitation that a family member often offers to me: When I am in a cycle of self-loathing, this family member will often say to me, "Be nicer to my friend Sean." While it's arguably the most annoying thing anyone says to me, it's also perhaps one of the most useful. So I ask you, too: "Be nicer to my friend ______. That person is doing the best they can."

Neural Exercise 6:
Taking Some Time to Be Kind to Yourself

Being kind to myself is really challenging, and my guess is it might be for you too. I could be wrong about that, but my assumption is that if you bought this self-help book, it's because you are looking for something to make life easier and better. So, to that end, let's do that unnatural thing of sitting with your dorsal and sympathetic activation and being kinder to my friend ______.

1. Think about a time you were happy, and just take a minute to trace your experience. See what sensations, if any, come up for you. For example, is there a sensation of expansion in your chest? Do your shoulders loosen?

2. As you notice these sensations, pick one, and explore it a little further. See if you can learn something new about this very real experience. For instance, if you picked a constricting in your esophagus, see if you can follow the ways the body twists, and notice how far you can follow it.

3. As you notice what are hopefully comfortable sensations, see if you can feel into what made you happy in this memory. Were you with loved ones? Were you experiencing a sense of gratitude or safety? As you recall the circumstances of this happy memory, you may notice your happiness deepening, and the physical sensations elicited by this memory may deepen as well. If this is the case, I invite you to spread this feeling to the rest of your body.

6

Offering Ourselves Compassion

If you ask people in my life about me, you might get different perspectives depending on who you ask. To my former partners, I'm ruthless. To my family, I'm the most warmhearted doofus they know. Their perspectives reflect their own experience of me relationally. Our bonds provide the relational context within which safety either can or cannot occur and often shape responses. So, what if lack of empathy were not a choice, but rather a reflection of (a) a nervous system in a chronic state of threat and (b) an underlying assumption of mistrust? As Maya Angelou says, "I am human, nothing human is alien to me" (Sanchez, 2013). In short, what if anyone can lack empathy if the right conditions are present? Are any of us innocent?

I'd like to share a medical record of mine, written in the early 2000s by a behavioral consultant named Michael. Michael came to my home to work with me when I was a child. Here are some of his observations found in my medical record:

Sean seems to show a deficiency in his ability to take on the perspectives of others. This deficit is not merely a selfish action; rather, he truly lacks the important skill of thinking about other people's thoughts, emotions, goals, and motives (this skill is referred to as having a theory of mind). During the summer, I implemented several "theory of mind" activities with Sean. Although he was able to complete such tasks, there were a few instances when I knew he was providing me with a "rote" answer and there was one task where he was clearly lost. This task required him to differentiate between the desire and the thoughts of someone else and then to identify the emotion of a person both before and after specific events. (Johnny is going to get a brownie for dessert. He doesn't know this. Johnny WANTS a brownie. Johnny thinks he is getting cake. How does Johnny feel? How does he feel when he actually gets the brownie?) Sean needed several prompts and cues on my part to understand this simple and pretend scenario. Imagine how difficult it must be for him when he is confronted with a real and complex social situation. Apparently, there are many real life examples of Sean behaving selfishly or seemingly without regard to other people's feelings. These behaviors are not malicious, they are simply expressions of an inability to consider and understand the thoughts of others.

I share this example because it illustrates how behavioral consultants, when delivering family interventions, tend to deliver behavioral treatments based on the needs and wishes of the parent(s). While this is often done in an effort to aid the child and meet his or her apparent social and communication challenges, it is still ultimately a system that orbits around the needs and perceptions of someone other than the Autist.

Based on this excerpt, it is evident that the behavioral consultant was taking cues from my parents about how difficult their experience of me was. As Michael states, "There are many real-life examples of Sean behaving selfishly." My parents' inherent perception of me was a child who had a complete disregard for the feelings, thoughts, motivations, and desires of others. I feel for my parents, but I also feel for child-Sean and for all of us who have been perceived through this lens of inherent incapacity. What if it isn't that simple?

We've discussed how a lack of empathy in Autists stems from a chronically aroused nervous system in conjunction with relationships that contain some element of threat, such as mistrust or hurt. I would argue that Michael's observations of me and my parents' feedback hint at both of these components. As you reflect on my familial experience, I invite you to think back on your own as well. Many of us may recall behavioral notes or teachers' comments that painted us as future criminals—notes that made condemning statements, such as that we lacked empathy or were so self-centered we would never find love. Yes, those uncomfortable and familiar stabs at your self-concept were made from an early age, and while they may have been made by people who were well-intended, you still carry those wounds to this day. And for that, I'm sorry; but I invite you to consider the two elements presented above and these two questions:

1. What state was your nervous system in?

2. What was the relational context in which these perceptions occurred?

I suspect that these questions may radically reshape your harsh perspective of yourself and may unlock some things that you have held for quite some time.

WHAT STATE WAS YOUR NERVOUS SYSTEM IN?

Below, we will look at autism through an activity called *Polyvagal Elements*. This is an activity I do with other clinicians, and it's a great way to think about how what is happening in a person's mind and body might be reflective of that person's autonomic state. It provides an alternative way to think about psychology that moves us away from the *Diagnostic Statistical Manual* (*DSM*), which speaks in immutable terms of labels and diagnoses, and toward a more flexible mindset that takes our changeable nervous system into account. In the table below, I lay out the polyvagal elements associated with each of the three branches of the vagus nerve.

DORSAL VAGAL SYSTEM	SYMPATHETIC NERVOUS SYSTEM	VENTRAL VAGAL SYSTEM
What it is: The part of the vagus nerve that is often associated with the collapse response (i.e. when a person feels shutdown). This is sometimes called hypoarousal, and tend to introduce a withdrawal or isolation from others.	**What is it:** The part of the vagus nerve responsible for activating mobilizing responses of fight and flight. Is present when a person is in either an avoidant, anxious, irritated, or threatening.	**What is it:** The part of the vagus nerve a person is in when they feel safe, emotionally regulated, and as if their needs are met.
Present moment elements: Feeling numb, depressed, zoned out, like dying, shamed, or trapped. Bodily experience might include slowed heartbeat, lack of energy, exhaustion, disconnection from one's mind and body, decreased eye contact, and trouble digesting food.	**Present moment elements:** Feeling anxious, worried, angry, irritable, rage, uneasy. Bodily experiences of fast heartbeat, increased blood flow, sweating, tightening body parts (fist of jaw), thought speed increasing, thoughts beginning to swirl, increased emotional reactivity, need for predictability, rumination.	**Present moment elements:** Feeling grounded, settled, calm, curious, mindful, and compassionate.

Polyvagal Elements

Before we look at autism through the lens of these polyvagal elements, let's try using them with a simpler diagnosis, like depression. According to the *DSM-5-TR*, *depression* includes the following symptoms: down or hopeless mood and behaviors like irritability, withdrawal, restlessness, difficulties with focusing, and low energy. Let's look at the polyvagal elements that correspond to each of these symptoms, and map the autonomic states onto these experiences.

Depressed   Dorsal

Hopelessness   Dorsal

Irritability   Sympathetic

Withdrawal   Dorsal

Restlessness   Sympathetic

Difficulty Focusing   Sympathetic

Low Energy   Dorsal

While depression can sometimes be shaped by sympathetic activation, such as when it manifests as irritability and restlessness, it also seems to be shaped a great deal by primarily dorsal elements. What happens when we try the same thing with autism? Per the *DSM-5-TR*, *autism* can be described symptomatically as: difficulty with social cues (e.g., eye contact, reading emotions of others); difficulty with reciprocal social relationships; and restrictive, repetitive patterns of interest and behaviors (e.g., rumination). Let's look at the polyvagal elements illustrated in the above figure and identify what these symptoms reflect.

Difficulty with social cues   Dorsal

Difficulty with reciprocal social relationships
Sympathetic and/or Dorsal

Rumination or restrictive, repetitive interests/ behaviors   Sympathetic

From a polyvagal elements lens, autism looks symptomatically both dorsal and sympathetic in nature, which is further supported by the 14 studies, conducted across five decades, that demonstrate that Autists tend to have higher resting heart rates than those without autism.

I invite you, then, to consider the possibility that your lack of empathy as a child was not your fault but, rather, the result of high cardiac activity in conjunction with a family unit, school system, or some other type of social environment in which you did not always feel safe. Perhaps your worst moments of failure to empathize occurred in the context of a heartbeat that greatly outpaced your peers', all while you tried to make sense of a confusing and overwhelming social universe that your nervous system may or may not have been equipped to handle. My hope is that you will find a greater degree of compassion for yourself, because your heart rate is autonomic—that is, it was out of your control. And what if, when considering the moments you might seem to lack empathy, we could consider this at least partly beyond what you or any other person might be able to control?

RELATIONAL CONTEXT

Keeping in mind the relational context wherein social behaviors like a lack of empathy occur, I invite you to consider again the story I shared of my own lack of empathy. In April of 2020, I was engaged to be married to a young woman who was kind, sweet, easy-going in nature, and beautiful. We had been together two and a half years, but one evening we had a fight, during which she said she was done. No preparation, no warning. This is the context around the hurtful email I sent her eight months later, on Christmas day, an email that lacked any concern or consideration for what her motives, thoughts, or feelings might have been. The relational context in which this occurred was a dynamic of betrayal in my life. I share this because it highlights how a relational context can color our behaviors, such as my regrettable email or perhaps even those actions referred to by Michael, the behavioral consultant.

What was the relational context in which actions you now regret occurred? Did a teacher repeatedly choose to ignore your needs, which were clearly stated in your Individualized Education Plan, prompting you to respond with ire? It's hard to know without knowing you personally, but I suspect your problems may not have started with you. However, it is your responsibility to heal and change, perhaps with these neural exercises or the help of a skilled therapist.

MAKING SENSE OF LACK OF EMPATHY

As we reflect on perhaps some of the more painful elements of being an Autistic adult with a legacy of lacking empathy, we encounter a history of dysregulation. While looking back on your past may be painful, I hope that this chapter and the neural exercises in this book, particularly the following exercise, will help you look on your younger self with more kindness—which, in turn, may allow you to treat your current self with more kindness too. In this next exercise, we are again focusing on mindfulness with the value of kindness. Recall, kindness is responding as gently and easily as we can, and this state can be achieved by attuning to our own autonomic nervous system and to the nervous systems of others (Inderbitzen, 2024). Thus, this is an invitation to consider some of your worst moments with the gentlest of care.

Neural Exercise 7:
Kind Eyes

Try to hold in your mind a moment in which you lacked empathy. Ideally this will be a memory from your younger years, but it does not have to be. Consider where you were, who you were with, and what you said. As you do, reflect on the words, "Be kinder to my friend _______ (insert your name here)." As you sense into this mantra, remember:

A. Being Autistic means you come to the table with a nervous system locked in a state of threat. Nothing about the world in which "little you" existed felt safe.

B. The relational context in which you demonstrated a lack of empathy may itself have prompted you to act in ways that made others uncomfortable. In other words, it wasn't your fault. You were not acting in a void—you were *re*acting to a certain relational context that held some element of threat.

Questions to consider:

1. What polyvagal elements were present in the moment you lacked empathy or remorse?

2. What was the relational context of the moment in which you lacked empathy? Did you cause this, or was it perhaps at least partially the responsibility of someone else?

3. What do you notice happening in this present moment, both in your body and your feelings? Take time to be in this space with gentleness and ease because this is likely a painful and powerful experience. Give it space to unfold. Repeat to yourself, "Be kinder to my friend _______________."

Neural Exercise 8:
A Polyvagal Map of the Present Moment

Referring to the Polyvagal Map, I invite you to map out the symptoms that you can identify in your present-moment experience and to see if you can determine which polyvagal elements are at play in your nervous system. These symptoms might be things like thought processes (e.g., thinking negative thoughts), somatic indicators (e.g., feeling relaxed in your muscles, tense in your chest), or feelings (e.g., anxiousness, numbness). See what symptoms you feel, and then match them with polyvagal elements.

Polyvagal Map

A. Symptom _____________   A. Polyvagal State _____________

B. Symptom _____________   B. Polyvagal State _____________

C. Symptom _____________   C. Polyvagal State _____________

D. Symptom _____________   D. Polyvagal State _____________

E. Symptom _____________   E. Polyvagal State _____________

Now that you have a map of your nervous system, let's see what you can map out about your current state.

1. Which polyvagal states do your symptoms fall under? Is one state more present than the others?

2. If your nervous system is primarily in a dorsal or sympathetic state, what do you need to do to bring it back to a ventral place? At this time, I invite you to experiment with the neural exercises you've discovered so far in this book. Choose one to practice now. Do any of your symptoms change?

7

Finding Safety

For much of this book, we've spent time exploring the seemingly endless experience of threat, the ways it shows up, the ways it affects us. But what about the thing we're after, safety? While the majority of the scientific community tells us that being Autistic stems from a difference in brain wiring, I come at it from a different perspective. Rather than believing my patterns of behavior to be the result of immutable brain structuring, I consider how my heightened cardiac activity affects my lived experience and how that, in turn, might shape my thinking. I'd like to illustrate this with a story.

Early in my career as a therapist (which was not so long ago, but a number of years can feel like forever in a therapist's life),

I worked in local school districts. To be honest, I wasn't very good at it. One day my clinical supervisor, Susan (who is lovely beyond measure), had an impromptu meeting with me. In her ever elegant and tactful way, she walked into my office and said, "Sean, I need to talk with you about an incident, but first about something you put in a chat."

I looked at her rather cross-eyed and, feeling uneasy, said, "Okay."

"Have I ever, in the time you've known me, not approached you with gentleness and ease, trying to understand where you are coming from?"

"No," I replied.

"Then I need you to know that when you assume something bad is going to happen because I need to meet with you to work through a problem, that hurts me. I take you seriously, and you are good at what you do, but sometimes we all need redirection; and when you assume that you are going to be 'in trouble,' it hurts me."

The emotion that her words elicited in me was deeply perplexing; so much so, in fact, that it brought me to tears. These were not tears of guilt or shame but of safety and relief, because Susan had presented me with a subtle and wonderful challenge to my way of anticipating the worst from the world. Susan, unlike all my prior supervisors, perceived all the ways in which I felt threatened and uneasy in my experience with work. It was like she had a bullshit meter that only picked up on pain and could see right through whatever walls and defenses I might put up. This was the first time in my life when I felt safe enough to cry and admit my own shortcomings in front of someone who had the power to fire me.

As we've discussed, this seems to be a pattern among Autistic nervous systems—threat is detected regardless of whether a threat actually exists, as was the case when Susan told me she had something to discuss with me and I assumed the worst. This tendency can lead to dangerous assumptions. Take, for instance, the work of Becca Lory Hector, an Autistic person and the director of training for the Association of Autism and Neurodiversity (AANE). Hector lays out five steps for taking on ableism in the workplace (Hector, 2024). Her fifth step illustrates how the Autistic community expects threat from those who are not Autistic:

5. Seek Support and Community—DO NOT ATTEND any informal meetings about the incident or meetings where you are outnumbered and without representation. Instead, try reaching out to peers, contacting a related support group, or seeking a therapist if needed. (Hector, 2024)

This excerpt from Hector's work suggests a long experience of pain in the workplace—it assumes threat. And while I do not wish to invalidate Hector's experience nor the reality of ableism in the workplace, I do want to highlight our tendency, particularly those of us with autism, to assume the worst. After all, I held this negative assumption even about Susan until the interaction I described earlier, which shifted something within me and created a felt sense of safety.

A felt sense of safety is rooted in believing in the good: the good in myself, the good in others, and ultimately the good in the world, as esteemed psychotherapist Deb Dana would describe it. She writes so eloquently in her book *Anchored* about how our beliefs parallel our nervous system states (think back to polyvagal elements in Chapter 6). Let's revisit Hector's statement with polyvagal elements in mind. Again, she writes, "DO NOT ATTEND any informal meetings about the incident or meetings where you are outnumbered and without representation." In terms of what she believes about herself, it's hard to know, but based on the unequivocal nature of her warning, it's probably something like "I'm not safe." Concerning what Hector believes about others (e.g., her employer) it's probably something to the effect of, "Based on my past experience (or perhaps the experience of people she has known) in work situations, other people are not safe." Finally, in terms of her beliefs about the world, I'd take from her statement the belief is something like, "Most employers are not sensitive to the needs of autistic employees." Finally, in terms of her *beliefs about the world,* I infer from her statement that her belief is something like, "Employers do not care about Autistic employees." To me, all these beliefs seem to reflect someone in their sympathetic state and to mirror emotions as described in polyvagal elements, like anxious, worried, angry, irritable, rageful, uneasy. Things not easily felt and yet totally informing a dire and destitute view of the world, precisely like mine was with Susan.

I would argue that this view is not very helpful in the pursuit of a felt sense of safety. It is rarely beneficial to enter an interaction assuming the other person is harmful. I share this knowing full well that employers can and do discriminate against Autistic employees, but having been on both the receiving and giving ends of this type of assumption, I can say that it limits one's ability to experience feelings of openness, capacity, curiosity, and expansion. Because expecting the worst causes these problems, I believe that it's important to cultivate optimistic fundamental beliefs about the world. Often, it's not easy at first to muster a belief that the world is a place where good things happen, but when space is made for this possibility, good things often do indeed unfold. We're then able to move past the pain that stems from living in a constant state of threat and become open to those beautiful, energetic experiences that we call "feelings." But to get here takes some work. Thankfully, the esteemed Pat Ogden has already laid a path for this work in her PEACE protocol.

WHAT IS THE PEACE PROTOCOL?

The PEACE protocol is a way of helping clients, primarily those with trauma, to work toward finding an experience of safety. For Ogden, the PEACE protocol is a way of helping clients manualize a practice called somatic resources, which are mindful experiences of locations in the body. She does this through a process that I find useful for teaching both Autistic and non-Autistic clients a way of experiencing safety that engages with the wisdom of the body, rather than attempting to "reason" a client into feeling safe. I encourage you to engage with the PEACE protocol exercise below regardless of whether you believe you've experienced trauma, because, just like a person who has experienced trauma, an Autist has a highly dysregulated nervous system, which the PEACE protocol can help regulate. To me, the PEACE protocol is very much a gift to us from Ogden and a very simple way to work toward resilience. There is a link to the original PEACE worksheet (sensorimotorpsychotherapy.org/peace-protocol-demo/) through the resources section of the Sensorimotor Psychotherapy Institute website.

HOW TO USE THE PEACE PROTOCOL
AS AN AUTISTIC ADULT

One of the challenges Autists may face with somatic tools like this one is how overwhelming it can be to begin to feel one's emotions. The PEACE protocol presents a five-step method to ease some of the overwhelm. It's a regulating strategy for slowing down one's experience of feeling by using the body as a rooting mechanism. The core principle here is that the body can be a coping tool if one can learn to be in it and with it. To begin, let's start by slowing down.

NEURAL EXERCISE 9: THE PEACE PROTOCOL
AND A GENEROUS ASSUMPTION

Step 1: Pause what you are doing to briefly identify your bodily signals.

If you are an Autistic person presently in a state of threat, your mind is likely racing a thousand miles per minute. Choosing a

Sensorimotor Psychotherapy™
PEACE
Resource Protocol
5 Steps to Modulate Activation & Build Resilience

P — Pause what you are doing to briefly identify bodily signals of unrest.

Maybe you feel muscle tension, weakness, shakiness, numbness, shallow, rapid breathing, fast heart rate.

E — Embody a somatic resource that feels supportive in your body in this moment.

Try combining them (e.g., Breathe & Lengthen spine; Make a Stop gesture & Ground).

A — Acknowledge the positive effects of the resource.

Maybe you sense more relaxation, settled energy, slower heart rate, deeper breath, softer eyes, less numbness, or more energy and alertness.

C — Concentrate your attention on the positive effects of the resource for 15 seconds or more.

Focusing attention on internal signals of ease fortifies a resourced state & helps rewire your brain.

E — Engage with your environment.

Look around, notice pleasant sights, sounds, & smells, feel the air on your skin, connect with a person or a pet, drink water, taste something you enjoy.

Somatic Resources:

- **Orient**, look around, name colors you see
- **Lengthen** your spine
- **Ground,** sense your feet connect with the earth
- **Breathe** slowly & lightly through your nostrils, into your belly
- **Place hands** on heart or belly, or hug yourself
- **Smile** in a way that feels right to you
- **Make a "Stop" gesture** with palms open, facing outward
- **Stand up**, feel your feet push against the floor
- **Push palms** of hands against each other, the wall, or an object
- **Hum** with a low pitch and sense the vibration
- **Move** rhythmically: rock, sway, bounce, swing
- **Walk** slowly, sensing your legs moving
- **Embody your culture**, its traditions, and/or the support of your ancestors

Sensorimotor Psychotherapy Institute

...because words are not enough

Find more resources at sensorimotorpsychotherapy.org

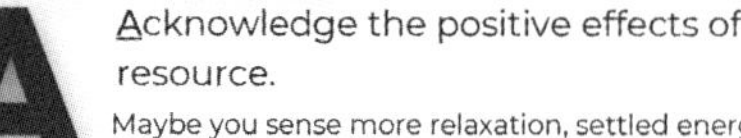

©Sensorimotor Psychotherapy Institute

PEACE Protocol

PEACE Resource Protocol by Pat Ogden and Sensorimotor Psychotherapy Institute

single body part to focus on can help release you from the prison of your mind. Do you notice your chosen body part tensing, loosening, shaking? Take a moment to tune in.

Step 2: Embody a somatic resource.

As you notice and tune into your bodily signals, refer to the Peace Protocol and, from the list in the box on the right side of the figure, pick a somatic resource that you think might feel good to you. Give it a try; and give it time to sink in. If that one doesn't work, pick another and try it out.

Step 3: Acknowledge the positive effects of the resource.

Taking the time to again just notice your body, see what helpful changes have occurred in your body after embodying the somatic resource(s); maybe your breath has slowed, some muscles have released or relaxed, etc. Take in deeply the effects of using this new resource.

Step 4: Concentrate on the positive effects for at least 15 seconds.

My hunch is that if you are anything like most of the Autistic adults I work with, your attention is probably really scattered. If that is the case, it's okay. Just gently bring your attention back to the positive effects of trying on the resource and, if needed, repeat the resource. The goal isn't perfection but rather to deepen your experience of the effects of the resource you are experimenting with.

Step 5: Engage with your environment.

After concentrating on the positive effects of the resource you practiced, take time to return to the present—not all at once, but slowly and steadily, as you are ready. Stay in the positive effects as long as you need to, but when you are done, come on out of that space.

Step 6: (Try to) Assume the best about someone else.

As I wrote in earlier chapters, generosity is a neural exercise value. Again, it can be understood as a stance that embodies "nonpossessive, sharing, acknowledgment, collaboration, cooperation" and "giving more than you receive" (MINT, n.d., as cited by Inderbitzen & Porges, 2024). Now that your nervous system has, hopefully, found some rest through the PEACE protocol, picture someone with whom you have a difficult relationship. Now think of a time when they irritated you, and make a generous assumption about why they did the thing that irritated you. Write it down. (And no, sorry; sarcasm doesn't count here.) The goal is to lean toward an assumption that the world is a fundamentally good place.

Neural Exercise 10:
Mapping Our Assumptions

Underlying pessimistic assumptions can breed mistrust and keep us very lonely. Consider the following:

A. As you read into my reaction to Susan's message that she needed to meet with me, sense into your nervous system. What part of the nervous system do my responses of mistrust of Susan evoke in your nervous system?

B. What beliefs about others, society, and the world come up when you read my initial response to Susan?

C. Reading the beliefs you wrote above and recalling that Deb Dana (2021) says our beliefs parallel our nervous system states, what type of nervous system states do your beliefs reflect?

8

The Fixing Reflex

I have a friend whom I'll call Sarah. Sarah is another Autist therapist, and I want to share her experiences when she was once handling a particularly challenging case that involved a client who was, allegedly, abusive to her son. Child Protective Services were involved, and there were allegations of bruises on the child. One day, Sarah received a call from her client, who asked, "Any chance we can have a session today? Things aren't looking good."

Sarah spent half an hour speaking with her client, who was suicidal, and by the end of their session, the client agreed to not end her life. Sarah acted exactly as she should have, contacting law enforcement and CPS and calling her supervisor to report the incident.

One night not long after, however, Sarah received a puzzling text message from her client, which read "Looks like I won't make it to our next session." Shortly afterward, she received a call from law enforcement reporting the death of her client. Her client had first taken her son into a hostage situation; the child had been released, but Sarah's client had taken her own life. Sarah dropped to the ground and the officer hung up.

Naturally, as therapists do, Sarah booked a session with her own psychologist, someone who specialized in treating therapists with clients who have taken their own lives.

"This is rough, huh?" the psychologist asked gently during their first session.

"Yeah," Sarah said, her tone flat.

"So tell me about what you are experiencing with this death you told me about on the phone."

"Not a whole lot of anything. I feel nothing."

"Well, what happens if you just stay with that nothingness?" the psychologist asked.

Sarah was resistant, but agreed to sit for a minute with her feeling of nothing. "There is this image of a small person," she said.

"Can you describe this person?"

"She's young, probably no more than 5 years old, and she feels guilty." Tears started to run down Sarah's face.

"Do you recognize this little girl?" the psychologist asked.

"Yes."

"What is she doing?"

"She wants to fix things before her mom gets home, because she knows what's coming."

"What's coming?"

Sarah's throat constricted such that it was difficult for her to speak. Pain surged through her back, and her tears came faster.

"Would it be okay with this little girl if we just stayed with her so we can see what she's scared of?"

Sarah nodded.

"If you could just reassure her that I am here with her, and so are you, I think that would be really helpful," the psychologist said.

Internally, Sarah turned toward this little girl and said, "It's okay if you can't fix it."

The tears came running down Sarah's face, and the psychologist said, "Even if you were the best therapist in the world, you never could have saved her. I saw the case file from CPS."

"I know, but I wanted to so badly."

"I know you did. But none of that is going to stop from happening what already happened to this little you, who just really wants to fix it, huh?"

"My mom used to take her anger out on me," Sarah said.

"So she really wants to fix things so that doesn't happen again, huh?"

"Yeah."

"Well, what if we just let her know that mom isn't coming, and maybe that she doesn't need to fix anything for her to be okay?"

PROTECTORS, RIGIDITY, AND THE FIXING REFLEX

What Sarah experiences in this example is known in the field of motivational interviewing as the *fixing reflex*—a clinician's urge to "fix" their client rather than holding space for their client's own empowerment and growth. While in the context of motivational interviewing, this term is specific to mental health clinicians, it's also a pretty common experience to want to fix our loved ones' problems rather than holding space for their emotions when they come to us for support. In Sarah's case, the urge to fix her client was driven by a protector part (using parts language) that wanted to fix *every* situation in order to protect Sarah. This fixing reflex (or "fix-it part") kept Sarah dissociative; instead of feeling her emotions, she tried to fix things. She was out of touch with her emotions until she met with that psychologist, who skillfully led her to confront the child part of her who was in so much pain.

In cognitive behavioral therapy language, this might be referred to as *black-and-white* thinking—thinking that is rooted in a dichotomous thought process (e.g., good or bad) and has a high level of intolerance for uncertainty. Sarah likely would not have been able to save her client no matter how much skill or experience she had as a therapist—but she was unable to tolerate the "gray space" created by knowing that she was unable to save her client *and* that she is still a good therapist who did everything she could. Her fix-it part functioned to resolve the ambiguity; but what Sarah's other, nonprotector parts needed from her adult Self was not for her to try to fix it, but rather to slow down long enough for her to feel her feelings.

The fixing reflex is one manifestation of rigidity that is often experienced by those with autism. Several studies demonstrate evidence of a high correlation between dichotomous thinking and autism (Stark et al., 2021; Shi & Hirai 2024; Suzuki & Hirai 2023; Hwang et al., 2020). Thus, it's common for Autists to experience black and-white thinking, and this thought pattern may very well show up as a protector part insisting that we "fix things."

This protector part may have served as an adaptive strategy for you; in some context, it kept you safe. However, it also serves a counter function: this rigidity in response to stress might reflect a desire to avoid feeling. It's often subtle, but the ability and propensity to stay in the reasoning mind and out of feeling one's feelings—that is, seeing things primarily through the lens of logic—is a way by which some Autists approach and organize the world. As we will discuss, however, logic cannot override the experience of pain. Pain is its own emotional experience that must be gone through—not around, over, or below. Pain can only be gone through and felt every step of the way.

SO, I'M PRETTY STUCK—WHAT NOW?

In this time, when access to affordable health care has never been more uncertain, you may be wondering what sort of neural exercises you can do on your own to reduce rigidity and the fixing reflex without the help of a therapist. The following neural exercises describe ways to get out of your "head brain" and into your "heart brain." These three applied neural exercises are useful for shaping and moving your inner world experience.

Neural Exercise 11: Connecting, Not Fixing

Think of a time when you were with a friend and they told you something challenging or painful for them. Imagine them coming to you with this dilemma, and try to answer the following questions while resisting the urge to fix. (The urge to fix or fixing reflex sounds like, "Well if you just do this, or fix that . . .")

1. As you envision this scenario, imagine this friend saying, "I just don't know what I'm going to do." Stop for a minute, and just notice what comes up for you. My hunch is, if you are anything like me, what comes up is an impulse to intervene or give an answer. Don't. Save yourself the trouble and stop trying to fix it. Instead, write down an open-ended question or a reflection that isn't a suggestion. This might sound like, "What's so hard about it?" or "You really don't know what you are going to do."

2. Hard, huh? It is for me. Imagine you ask that question and they go on to say, "Yeah, it's really hard. I wish I could have some idea of what to do." Again just stop and notice. Write down what comes up for you. It's okay if it's advice.

3. Now try something really novel: I want you to seek permission from this person before you give advice; if they say okay, then you can. Write down the way you want to ask permission to offer advice. Again this might sound something like, "Would it be okay if I shared something with you?" This may feel unnatural, and that's okay.

4. Finally, you can go ahead and give your advice. Let us, for the exercise, assume your friend is okay with it; now you can go ahead. Write down what you've been wanting to say all along.

The fundamental purpose of this exercise is about generating some slowness and patience over the course of all four questions, not just about getting unstuck in the moment. Yes, this might feel like a trick, but we know people on the spectrum struggle with inhibition, so this is a way of taking that sympathetic system and ratcheting it down some notches to be more ventral in orientation.

Neural Exercise 12:
Getting Connected to Yourself

Many of the neural exercises in this book are designed to get you out of your head brain and into your heart brain. This exercise has the same goal. It involves, however, the challenging work of knowing yourself in a way that may not be comfortable. In fact, some of my clients use the word "irritating" to describe this process. However, this exercise involves sensing into some of the ways you get when you try to feel or maybe feel without thinking about it.

1. Take a moment to settle into your seat. Get comfortable, and as you do, pick a feeling and see if you can call it to mind. When you try to describe this feeling to yourself, what words come up? Write them below.

2. If you are anything like most of my clients, or even me, actually naming what you are feeling is difficult, perhaps even annoying. I recommend you stick to simple emotion words (e.g., happy, angry, sad, glad, disgusted, or afraid). Without overanalyzing the feeling, see if one or some of these simple words describe what you are experiencing. Write your emotion words below.

3. As you read your chosen emotion word(s), write down what it's like internally when you try to capture this experience. What is your experience of describing your emotions? Maybe refer to things in energetic words, like openness or discomfort. It's okay if what you feel aren't positive emotions. Generally, negative emotions are harder to be with. Harder emotions are worth bonus points because we are often taught it's not okay to feel these. Truthfully, it is okay to feel all your feelings.

4. As you sit with your description of the feeling, spend time exploring what sensations your body or parts of your body are experiencing. Body parts that tend to hold a lot of energy include the stomach, heart, lungs, and arms. Explore sensation words, pick the ones that describe your inner world experience, then write them below.

9

Vulnerability and Feeling

The impulse to heal is real and powerful and lies within the client. Our job is to evoke that healing power, to meet its tests and needs and support it in its expression and development. We are the context in which healing is inspired.

—RON KURTZ, *BODY-CENTERED PSYCHOTHERAPY* (2009), AS CITED BY OGDEN, 2021

In the movie *Good Will Hunting,* Robin Williams portrays a therapist who tells a brilliant but challenging young man (played by Matt Damon), "But you've never looked at a woman and been totally vulnerable. Known someone that could level you with her eyes" (Van Sant, 1997). What I love about this scene is how Williams's character frames the experience of being undone. I recently experienced something similar when my friend Beth told me, "Sean, you're a blessing, not a burden." With these six words, she managed to waltz past all my defenses. What Williams eludes to in *Good Will Hunting,* and what I experienced in this anecdote, is *vulnerability.*

Vulnerability, as Brené Brown defines it, is "risk, uncertainty, and emotional exposure" (Brown, as cited by Jensen, 2019). She goes on to state, "to love is to be vulnerable, to give someone your heart and say, 'I know this could hurt bad, but I'm willing to do it; I'm willing to be vulnerable and love you'" (Brown, as cited by Jensen, 2019). That is, to invite the possibility for one's heart to be shattered into a thousand pieces and simultaneously to be open to the possibility of experiencing deep happiness. This is what it is to be, as Williams says, "leveled by her eyes."

For me, the phrase, "You're a blessing, not a burden" invites vulnerability. All in the span of six words, my walls came down, and through her words, she reached out and invited my most terrible ways of being into the light, into a space where even the darkest, coldest, and most calloused parts of me are welcome. Parts of me that hold such deep pain, shame, and guilt inevitably will be my undoing if I cannot hold space for them. And around her, they come out. Feel seen. Feel heard. So, you may be wondering, how does a person do that? With just the glance of their eyes, or the turn of a phrase?

While I can't tell you for sure, I think as we cultivate vagal efficiency, we encounter certain people who, as Kurtz states, meet "the tests and needs for support and development of expression" (Kurtz, as cited by Ogden, 2021). That is, our darkest edges might begin to feel safe enough to let down their well-oiled defensive strategies in the context of those who bring our nervous system into a certain level of harmony. To unpack this mysterious process, in this chapter, we will explore all the ways we experience safety—and how developing a felt sense of safety is not a matter of consciousness but rather one of neuroception, or a preconscious felt sense of safety. We will explore music, beauty, nature, and more to begin to unpack this experience and perhaps draw up some tools.

When my book *Autism in Polyvagal Terms* was published, my eldest son, Shean, all of 10 years old, was with me in the car listening to me talk to his grandfather. We were chatting about Beth. Thinking nothing of it, we went to Shean's soccer tournament and then onto my book-launch party at Two Roots (Eau Claire, WI). There, I was chatting with this woman I had been talking about, and up walks Shean, and in his ten-year-old wisdom says, "Hi Beth, I'm Shean."

"Nice to meet you Shean, I'm Beth, a friend of your dad's."

"Oh, my dad was talking to my grandpa about you on the phone today."

"Oh . . . he was? Tell me all about what he said."

As you might imagine, I was dying inside, but on went my very energetic and open 10-year-old, telling Beth about his dad's thoughts. And while Shean had no idea what he was doing (to the best of my knowledge), the sense I have about this interaction is how unready I generally am to be seen. Embarrassed, if you will, but perhaps this is what it is to be Autistic and to feel chronically in threat. When one is chronically in threat, it can be deeply unsettling the first time we find ourselves outside of that milieu of threat—to be in a place where we feel dismantled by someone's eyes and yet completely okay and embraced by the sense of warmth it generates within us.

SITTING WITH UNCOMFORTABLE FEELINGS

Feeling requires a degree of willingness on our part to be open to it, a strong ventral vagal system. This is something that people with autism tend to struggle with—we often use the term *alexithymia* to describe this phenomenon. As discussed in a previous chapter, alexithymia means, "difficulty identifying and describing one's feelings, and externally oriented patterns of thinking" (Nemiah et al., 1976).

And so, while much of this book has been geared toward learning ways to cope with rigidity and to increase one's sense of safety, this chapter is devoted to learning to be in the center of feelings that might evoke tension or discomfort. The word we therapists use for this process is *titrating*; in this context, titrating is to begin to sit with and move in and out of something that might be somatically, cognitively, or even emotionally discomforting. With the expanded vagal efficiency we are developing by flipping the vagal switch through neural exercises, we begin to learn to live in the middle of this discomfort and to be better prepared to tolerate what might feel very foreign.

MAKING SPACE FOR THE GOOD AND THE BAD

In her 2016 song "Can't Keep My Hands to Myself," Selena Gomez sings, "Cause all of the uppers and downers make love to each other." This line seems to suggest tension between her and an alleged lover—a tension that, while overwhelming, is simultaneously pleasurable. Similarly, sometimes flipping the vagal switch isn't about resolving the tension but rather about widening our ability to tolerate the energetic experience of emotions to deal with the simultaneous frustration and pleasure of them. It is in this internal conflict that we can make ourselves vulnerable and can titrate in and out of the discomfort and simultaneous deep joy. In widening our access to the ventral vagal system, we begin to encounter where reason ends and the logic of feelings begins.

My interactions with Beth, as described above, fall into this category of my own greater capacity for feeling, achieved through flipping the vagal switch. It is as if the light gets incrementally brighter, and to the nervous system, it becomes easier and easier to tolerate that light, but on the flipside, it is painful. The pain of tolerating more and more energetic expression is a bit like exercising a muscle; just like lifting weights brings some measure of discomfort, some amount of pain comes with this use of unfamiliar emotional musculature. Let's return for a moment to Beth's phrase, "You are a blessing, not a burden." For me, this phrase actually evokes a great deal of pain, because to my mind, "I am the patron saint of lost causes," as the band Anberlin coined in their song, "Dismantle. Repair." (Anberlin, 2007). And so, when Beth says that I'm someone she wants to be around and that even my messy parts evoke a sense of warmth and welcoming in her, I'm challenged to see myself as something more than broken.

In other words, it is challenging for me to see how uniquely wonderful I am. The discomfort or growth edge Beth's perception of me elicits is captured in Anberlin's song when they sing, "You dismantle me down. Repair." (Anberlin, 2007). "Growth edge" refers to areas of life that challenge us to grow and increase our capacity for anything, but in this case, vulnerability. In the context of this book and of relational safety, I use *growth edge* to refer to moments in which we find ourselves with another person whose perception of us dismantles our own, someone who sees our pain as something far more beautiful than we experience, ourselves.

I expect you may have experienced a great deal of pain over the course of your life. And if so, that's okay. I think that's why Autists so regularly like to criticize behaviorists who deliver applied behavioral analysis (ABA) to them. To date, ABA has a fair number of critics, but in my opinion, most of the studies conducted so far have methodological limitations that weaken the argument that ABA is traumatizing to people like me. If you want to know more about why I think so, I'd recommend that you listen to my interview on *Behavior Bitches* on March 17, 2025, which is called "Autism, Polyvagal Theory & the ABA Debate with Sean Inderbitzen," and which you can find here: https://behaviorbitches.com/podcast/behavior-bitches-autism-polyvagal-theory-the-aba-debate-with-sean-inderbitzen/. However, as we can see through my example with Beth and how difficult it was for me to be told that I'm a blessing in her life, a behavioral consultant who is careless in his endorsements might produce lasting harm for

Autists. What Michael didn't know about me—that which Beth does see in me, so she says—is that when I have access to my ventral vagal system (i.e., when my nervous system is in a state of safety), I do not lack the capacity to be empathetic. Sometimes it takes the right person—in my case, Susan or Beth—to allow us to reach that state of safety. But we also must be open to the possibility that other people can be that source of light and warmth for us; in other words, *we have to be vulnerable.* And being vulnerable requires its own baseline of safety. It's like a ladder: by working through these neural exercises, we can increase our felt sense of safety, which can allow us to be open and vulnerable, which can open the door to letting in people who can help us to feel even more safe. It can—and probably will—hurt to be vulnerable and let people in because, by definition, being vulnerable means giving another person the power to hurt us. But it also allows us to feel the deep joy that comes from relationships of all types. To begin this work, I invite you to develop deeper acceptance and compassion for your particular growth edges.

APPLYING ORGANICITY TO CULTIVATE SAFETY

As previously discussed, organicity, within the context of a disordered nervous system, is to consciously, intentionally, make an assumption of positive intent, which then shapes our responses, helping them derive less from a dorsal and/or sympathetic state and more from a ventral vagal state. In terms of neuroception for Autists, organicity develops from an applied neural exercise designed to nurture and perpetuate a perspective that more resembles that of a nondysregulated nervous system. Often, safety can be realized within the context of a relationship. Again, it requires vulnerability, which involves a great deal of risk and depends on a certain amount of established vagal efficiency. Through the neural exercises in this book, we can begin to build enough access to the ventral vagal system to begin to tolerate our feelings and understand their meaning. Though tension-invoking, the exercises can produce a greater sense of grace and wonder toward one's Autistic Self. When we nourish our sense of Self through the lens of "you are a blessing, not a burden," we begin to dismantle our best defenses around being seen. And it is only when we allow ourselves to be seen—by others and by ourselves—that we can deeply and richly experience the fullness of who we are. And while one could fill an entire book with neural exercises that we may need to overcome the hurdles placed by our most protective parts, those that assist us so well in trying to not be seen, here we simply begin to apply the value of organicity to the goal of feeling seen.

Neural Exercise 13:
"You're a Blessing, Not a Burden"

In your mind's eye, picture for a moment someone who evokes in you a sense of safety. Take in the aspects of this person, and just stay in this feeling for a few moments. Really pause with it. If you can, fully embrace that person's presence. As you do, hear them say the words, "You're a blessing, not a burden." What comes up for you when you hear them say this?

Below, write about your experience imagining that person saying "You're a blessing, not a burden."

Did you encounter any emotions that you were not expecting when you imagined a loved one saying this mantra? Write about it/them below.

If you encountered some discomfort with this mantra, consider it as a probe. Imagine again this person who makes you feel welcomed and seen. And as you do, imagine them asking you, "What is so dysregulating about the phrase, 'You're a blessing, not a burden'?"

FINDING A THERAPIST TO HELP YOU DEVELOP VULNERABILITY

> It's always a risk to take action. It might not work, it might blow up in your face, you might lose money, you might fail. No one may get it. But that's not the only risk. There's another risk: the risk of not trying it . . . of continuing in the same direction in the same way, wondering about other paths and possibilities, believing that this is as good as it gets while discontent gnaws away at your soul.
>
> —ROB BELL, *HOW TO BE HERE*

I like this quote because it captures the 33 years of numbness and nonfeeling I experienced before building vagal efficiency. Autism can be very disordering for me; and it's within this context that I've tried to help my patients as well as other mental health clinicians who work with people like me. Much of my mission in this work has centered on working with clinicians so that they are more willing to work with people with autism.

A great deal of the debate around the topic of what is the right way to serve Autistic people or decide what we call them has largely been focused on what I consider to be the wrong issues. Access to mental health care is not a certainty, and to assume the opposite is naïve. Perhaps best highlighted by Brenna Maddox and colleagues at UPenn in 2019, only 2 in 44 therapists in the greater Philadelphia area were willing to treat adults with autism (Maddox et al., 2020). This finding has been replicated in other studies (Unigwe et al., 2017; Ghaderi & Watson, 2019; Gallant et al., 2023). My thought is that therapists' willingness to work with Autistic folks can be increased by improving their confidence levels.

What makes a good therapist has nothing to do with what language they use, what protocol they adhere to, nor what specific ingredients they use in therapy. It's actually far simpler. In my eyes, what makes a good therapist is their openness to being told what is and is not working for their clients. Drawing from the work of Wampold, this is the central tenet of the Feedback Informed Treatments Session Rating Scale concept developed by Scott Miller, PhD, Barry Duncan, and colleagues. On this scale, therapists are not encouraged to try to achieve perfect scores of 40 out of 40 (Duncan & Miller, 2000) with clients, but, rather, to see how close they can get to an imperfect 36. They do this by asking their clients to score them in real-time, using a ten-point scale, regarding elements of what the therapist did that did and did not work for them, the client. This immediate, real-time feedback is useful for discussing possible modifications (see Neural Exercise 14 for my version of the session rating scale).

You can really begin to assess the level of safety you have with another person by your own willingness to offend their sensibilities. Neuroception (one's felt sense of safety) creates space for differences and openness to being wrong, and this is what a good therapist will give you: the space to question their judgments, to entertain disagreement, and to challenge your thinking, because sometimes we need those things in order to develop. Examples of how a therapist might hold space for your feedback include them asking you about their performance, asking questions that sound like, "What didn't work for you today?" or asking other open-ended questions that facilitate you expressing disapproval of their performance.

So, yes, engaging in effective therapy begins with the risk of you offending your clients and your clients offending you, because it means doing the work of forging a relationship with someone who likely is going to create tension. Again, the challenge may well be finding a therapist who is both open to feedback and willing to work with clients with autism. I do not assume that every reader will have access to such a therapist. However, Neural Exercise 14 is really intended to be done with a therapist who is open to feedback, so it is with cautious optimism that I invite you to consider this practice. Because this exercise is a bidirectional practice of honesty that may create some tension, I recommend against practicing it with a loved one. Really, any good licensed mental health care practitioner will do (if not a therapist, then a nurse, a psychiatric nurse practitioner, a psychiatrist, your case manager, etc.). The questions in the exercise, derived from the Feedback Informed Treatment Session Rating Scale (Duncan et al., 2004) are meant to be used as a tool for you to practice giving someone feedback.

Neural Exercise 14:
Eliciting Safety by Sharing Feedback

For this neural exercise, begin by sharing with your provider (therapist, ideally) that you are practicing vulnerability in sharing honest feedback to help them help you better in therapy.

You are going to rate them across four areas, trying to rate at least one of these areas below a ten; and then, if you feel safe enough, provide a rationale as to why. While the point of this exercise is to be vulnerable, if sitting with your therapist and completing all the steps together is too overwhelming, it is okay to write out your feedback, give it to your therapist for their reaction, and then discuss your feedback together later. Again, the goal of this exercise is to *not* give your therapist or practitioner a perfect score (40/40). If you find you have given them a perfect score, you probably have missed the mark for this exercise and have not yet made progress on increasing your vulnerability; so try again!

Read and complete in front of your provider the following statements:

1. On a scale of 1 to 10, I believe you scored a _____ today in terms of making me feel seen, connected to, and known, with 10 being most and 1 being least.

   If you feel comfortable, supply your provider with a rationale for why you gave them this score, and give them a chance to react by asking, "What do you make of my feedback?"

2. On a scale of 1 to 10, I believe you scored a _____ today in terms of focusing on what I wanted to focus on and work through, with 10 being most and 1 being least.

If you feel comfortable, provide your provider with a rationale for why you gave them this score, and give them a chance to react by asking, "What do you make of my feedback?"

3. On a scale of 1 to 10, I believe you scored a _____ today in terms of the fitness of how you work with me in the therapy space, with 10 being most and 1 being least.

   If you feel comfortable, provide your provider with a rationale for why you gave them this score, and give them a chance to react by asking, "What do you make of my feedback?"

4. On a scale of 1 to 10, I believe you scored a _____ today in terms of what I got out of this session, with 10 being most and 1 being least.

   If you feel comfortable provide your provider with a rationale for why you gave them this score, and give them a chance to react by asking, "What do you make of my feedback?"

Neural Exercise 15:
Glimmers

Glimmers are the little joys and wonders we find in our world that remind our nervous system that we are safe. For example, a glimmer for you might be a beautiful sunset, the first sip of your morning coffee, or snuggling with your dog. Polyvagal pioneer Deb Dana developed the concept of glimmers, and the concept is based on Polyvagal Theory and the idea that we can experience neuroception (a felt sense of safety) when our nervous system is in a ventral state. Glimmers are around us every day, but we may not notice them because of our negativity bias (our brain's propensity to focus on threat). When we practice intentionally noticing glimmers, however, we can train ourselves to become more easily aware of them on a daily basis; and experiencing these micromoments of safety more frequently can contribute to a more regulated nervous system.

This, in turn, can help us feel safe enough to be vulnerable to feeling our emotions.

To that end, I invite you to take a moment to consider some glimmers that you experienced this week. If you're having trouble coming up with any, try thinking of things you're grateful for. Write your glimmers from the past week below.

What are two sensations that show up in your nervous system and body as you consider the past week's glimmers? Are there any feelings that accompany them?

Neural Exercise 16:
Top-Down Wisdom

As you read the quote below, trace what thoughts come up for you. In this book, we spend a lot of time doing bottom-up processing (that is, working from the body), but occasionally top-down wisdom (cognition) has something valuable to offer. Consider again the Rob Bell quote from earlier in the chapter:

It's always a risk to take action. It might not work, it might blow up in your face, you might lose money, you might fail. No one may get it. But that's not the only risk. There's another risk: the risk of not trying it . . . of continuing in the same direction in the same way, wondering about other paths and possibilities, believing that this is as good as it gets while discontent gnaws away at your soul. —*Rob Bell,* How to Be Here

1. What is something "big" that you are considering acting on?

2. What, if any, are the risks of acting?

3. What are the risks of not acting?

4. Sensing into your nervous system, what do you notice comes up when you think about not acting on this big decision?

5. Sensing into your nervous system again, what do you notice comes up when you think about taking action?

In completing this exercise, I suspect you may have experienced more than mere thoughts—you likely had bodily reactions of some kind as you weighed your options. Part of why it's important to ask yourself these types of questions and work top-down is to see how connected our sensations, feelings, and thoughts are. Our beliefs about the world, as we explored in Neural Exercise 10, are often linked to the experience of our nervous system, which is in a body.

I hope you are now starting to be suspicious of our friend René Descartes, because what he doesn't account for—and which Polyvagal Theory and most modern interpersonal neurobiology-influenced psychotherapies do capture—is that we live in a body. And the body has a tremendous amount of influence on shaping our nervous systems' experience of our cognition.

10
· ·

Tolerating Discomfort

Vance Joy is my son Shean's favorite musician, and "Like Gold" is one of his better works, in my opinion. As is often the case with songs, what I find meaningful about "Like Gold" is how I experience it in relation to my personal life. I heard this song a lot in July of 2021, the same month a girlfriend left me. At the time, I was still unlearning many habits we had formed, and so the song's chorus "Gold when you see me; Hi, if you need me" particularly resonated with me, as I was unclear if my ex was friend or enemy, if she was coming or going. When I stumbled across this song, these words fully captured the lack of orientation I was experiencing in my life.

Four years later, this song came up again in the shuffle of my music library, with the words, "Babe, that's the way it was. That's the history. Blue, how we used to roar. Like an open fire. That's the way it was." What was once so confusing is now nothing more than a memory, a distant experience of lack of clarity. My world, more defined and grounded, remains settled despite the occasional upset. My ex never came back, and I have, more or less, moved on. My boys have grown years older, and this sad, disorienting time has faded. And now the words, "Blue, how we used to roar," aren't dark like an ocean but light like the sky on a summer day. This is the nature of memory and how we recall things; what in one moment is painful and unthinkable and seemingly insurmountable can later become simple. We usually (eventually) reach a place where the memory of that intolerable time can be looked back on with greater ease and depth. This, too, is what it means to flip the vagal switch. Habitually moving your nervous system from a place of dorsal collapse to a place of ventral safety opens us to possibilities that are not so grim and unending.

As I've alluded to, social scenarios, especially romantic ones, are typically not a person with autism's strong suit. Everything about these scenarios seems to fall into gray areas, which don't fit nicely into boxes and are thus a bit disruptive to my expectations. Unlike business, writing books, or even practicing therapy, it's difficult for me to map out how a romantic partner might react. And so, given my experience with past romances ending rather traumatically, I find myself rather shut off (in a dorsal state, if you will) to the possibility of allowing someone new in. For instance, on one occasion of asking someone to dinner,

I experienced a full blown panic attack: weak knees, feeling like I was going mute, and the sense I was going to throw up. To phrase it in the language of parts, this managerial part of me that manifested as a panic attack is not fearful of the other person's rejection; no, it expects that. Rather, the possibility of success is far more terrifying. This part of me is terrified at the idea that someone can want me, take the time to get to know me and all my weird idiosyncrasies—my love of Starbucks and pop-punk concerts, and even my refusal to have a TV because I think that all the best things happen in the present, "real life" moment.

The notion that someone could actually get to know all these weird little things that make Sean "Sean" and then wake up one day and decide to "peace out" is terrifying. In the context of asking someone to dinner, the person saying yes, the two of us hitting it off, and then it ending is a grim but perfectly normal possible outcome. But it is the nature of the sympathetic system to get one revved up for possible danger.

This example highlights how the fear of possibility—or sympathetic arousal—can increase rigidity and cause us to enter a dorsal state that disconnects us from the possibility of deep and meaningful connection. For me, the possibility for deep connection would mean allowing someone to come near enough to actually get to know me. I was thwarted by my own protective parts, which produced the panic-like sequence of symptoms: weak knees, shaking, shallow breathing. These are expressions of my nervous system's sense that my life is in danger. This beautiful protector would have saved my life 10,000 years ago on the African savannah. But this instinctual form of survival that kept our ancestors alive now becomes activated in a way that prevents me from accepting bids for connection: friendly conversations, smiles. Due to my conscious and subconscious memories of pain from past relationships, signals that should be perceived as signals of welcoming and openness are instead perceived as signals of danger or a potential predator.

Memory is an element that, up until this chapter, I haven't discussed but that directly influences our perception and in preconscious ways affects our sense of safety. This woman at the gym I wanted to ask to dinner had done nothing but be kind and discuss concerts and travel with me. But my historic experience kicked my nervous system first into sympathetic arousal, making it difficult to speak, and then into dorsal arousal, resulting in my missing a bid for romantic connection. Along the plane of possibilities, with greater flexibility and access to my ventral vagal state, my nervous system might have been more readily able to mirror hers—able to invite connection and maybe go to that place my protectors so desperately want to avoid.

AVOIDING SUFFERING

Suffering, in the story above and the other stories in this book, tends to stem from a dysregulated nervous system that is constantly on the lookout for threat. And as we've discussed, it's common for Autists' nervous systems to be overly prepared for threat in this way, which can result in thoughts that race a mile per minute and impulsive actions that follow those whirlwind thoughts. What can reduce suffering for us Autists, then, is slowing down.

But, as we discussed in Chapter 8, slowing down does not necessarily mean resolving the tension. No, slowing down includes sitting both with and in the tension in the body—that is, it involves sitting in our sympathetic states of arousal in order to downregulate our nervous system. By flipping the vagal switch, we are more readily able to arrive at a place where we can transcend the tension and move through it along the plane of possibility.

For me, this might look like moving through the panic and asking a woman to dinner; but for you, the reader, this might look different. What is it? What is that thing that evokes such great tension and rigidity in you that your only response is to shut down and become inaccessible to that bid for connection? Maybe you are like me, paralyzed by memories and thus highly dysregulated and unable to step into that fluorescent light in order to talk to a mysterious someone across the room. Maybe the harsh glare of the lights is intense enough for you to call it a day and subsequently beat yourself up for this failed bid at romantic connection—because you so deeply want to be seen and heard, but your stupid nervous system is unable to tolerate the way the light hits your eye.

Flipping the vagal switch won't stop the way light hits your eye (for example), but it can broaden your ability to tolerate the discomfort it causes—the tension it can create in your muscles, the momentary pressure in your body, or the nausea. Using the exercises in this book can be your pathway toward a more flexible experience that allows for more connections, romantic or otherwise. Pat Ogden, PhD, and Dan Siegel, MD, have named this space in which we can tolerate emotional dysregulation the "window of tolerance." This term is really another way of referring to the ventral vagal system, and the window of tolerance can become wider through practicing neural exercises. However, the window can retract in size as we encounter peaks of dysregulation along the plane of possible outcomes (e.g., me asking out the woman at the gym). However, with positive reinforcement, the window of tolerance can become broader, such that you are more able to withstand emotional experiences (e.g., fear of the unknown) and you remain able to tolerate and withstand the tension. So, the solution is not in avoiding suffering by flipping the vagal switch, it is in learning how to exist within and through suffering.

LIVING WITHIN AND OUTSIDE THE WINDOW OF TOLERANCE

I find that Autists are great at rejecting the notion that we are suffering. I'm not clear if this is always a strength, but it certainly can be. As I outlined in the author's note, one of the experts I have encountered calls autism an identity because it allows them to identify with other people like themself. They find that Autists can be a source of strength, given their mutual embracing of being particular and understanding that they are the experts on themselves, and that to violate this notion is to be oppressive. I, however, find this approach wanting.

As previously discussed, rigidity is an expression that is sympathetic in nature. It does serve a function, but in the context of the plane of possible connections that one can make, it is very limiting. Being unable to change and meet the needs of others results in isolation from others because it creates a barrier to connection. This is not to say that there are no instances in which advocating for oneself as an Autist is helpful; it is just that, in my eyes, a person who has a wider window of tolerance will tell you that not every battle is worth fighting. This inability to choose one's fights is, to me, a direct reason to be leery of anyone who says "the world needs to change because I have autism," and then offers some theory to back up why they are right.

Gabor Maté's critique of pathology, in his *New York Times* bestseller, *Myth of Normal*, argues that people are told they are disordered because of the disorder, and then cite the symptoms as the cause of the disorder. An example of this "logic" is, you are sad, unmotivated, sleepy, and not hungry because you have depression. You are diagnosed with depression because you are sad, unmotivated, sleepy, and lack an appetite. I view this circular reasoning as no different than when an Autist who contends that neurotypical people need to be more flexible with Autists then when under criticism for being inflexible states, "I'm inflexible because I'm Autist." Rigidity and sympathetic arousal that looks like restrictive, repetitive patterns of interest and behavior across the plane of possibility are in fact just this: nothing more than an inability to cope with change.

Often, Autists are unwilling and inflexible on occasions when we probably should be more flexible. In my case, those occasions tend to be Individualized Education Plan meetings, frustrating workplaces, and gym settings. Probably Autists all can name a few times we would like (if we could go back in time) to have been a bit more flexible with our friends, coworkers, teachers, or romantic partners. We can all probably think of a time when it might have been better if we had declined to fight a battle. To me, this demonstrates a lack of willingness on my part, a current inability to practice exercises that would help me meet the deep sense of longing that often goes unmet when I allow my busy mind and overactive cortex to be in charge.

The neurodiversity perspective that everyone around Autistic individuals needs to change (rather than the Autist) is useful for ignoring one's own suffering. This perspective refuses to admit when one is in pain and declines to consider ways to alleviate one's own suffering. As I've said before and will say again, autism, in polyvagal terms, can change over time. Thus, I take the position of optimism that you can coexist with your suffering and eventually move through it for greater and deeper types of connection.

None of this can be achieved by exclusively assuming the worst in others and remaining in a state of sympathetic arousal. This is not to say that sympathetic arousal, or a fight response that induces rigidity, has no place. No, some of the greatest moments in human history depict people unwilling to cave or "bend the knee." For example, in 1985, Nelson Mandela refused to accept the South African government's offer of conditional release from his prison cell in Cape Town, stating, "I cannot sell my birthright, nor am I prepared to sell the birthright of the people to be free" (Parks, 1985).

The difference, of course, between Mandela's refusal to embrace apartheid and someone advocating for themself against a special education department's applied behavioral analysis approach is context. The work you're engaging in throughout this book will allow you to have greater flexibility and a clearer sense of your own needs. For, as I have explained throughout this book, flipping the vagal switch and learning to identify what we are emoting, thinking, remembering, or even sensing in our inner worlds can unlock all kinds of relational possibilities when we begin to identify what we are emoting, thinking, remembering, or even sensing in our inner worlds. As Autists our possibilities become greater as we exit a state of dysregulated arousal and enter the plane of the ventral vagal system.

CONSIDERING THE LILIES

One of my favorite stories and one that I deeply relate to is the story of Emily Dickinson writing about her faith in a letter, stating, "The only Commandment I ever obeyed—'Consider the Lilies'" (Dickinson, 1894). While nowhere in this text have I promised to eliminate your suffering, I do offer you greater levels of openness and the ability to connect. And so the natural question that arises is: What is one to do with all this suffering? We both know that you didn't pick up this book because things were going particularly wonderfully; it's likely you were struggling. So, my answer to you is in the form of a neural exercise; this one is derived from traditional social work pedagogy.

The following practice focuses on returning one's attention to the present moment to remain grounded. Therapists do similar exercises to teach budding social workers how to detach from highly emotionally activating experiences so they may continue to navigate and remain professional in very painful situations (e.g., delivering to a parent the news that you must permanently remove their legal power to make decisions for and regarding their children). This tool, originally posted by differentbrains.org, is a great resource for learning to create some emotional distance from your thoughts and your feelings and to shift your nervous system into a ventral vagal state. By flipping your vagal switch, you will begin to learn how to move through suffering and determine whether a fight is worth the concomitant suffering.

Neural Exercise 17:
Considering Your Lily

Step 1

Notice your signals of distress in your body. These might be fast heartbeat, shallow breaths, racing thoughts, fast speech, or tightness in your chest.

Step 2

Using your five senses, look around the room for something that strikes awe and beauty in you. This is your *lily*. Pick one of your five senses to deeply explore this sense of wonder.

Step 3

Notice how the distress signals in your body change. Maybe your heart slows down or your breath deepens.

Step 4

Take 20 seconds to fully appreciate the beauty of your lily and to sink into the sense of ease and release.

Step 5

Re-engage with your surroundings and return to the present moment, carrying with you the full effects of observing your lily.

Step 6

Consider the following two questions:

1. Can I think of a different response to a situation that perhaps was not previously accessible to me?

2. If I can't come up with a different response, is this fight really worth any displeasure the fight causes if I end up not achieving the outcome I long for?

Neural Exercise 18:
Sensing From Your Nervous System

I'm a sucker for music, if you haven't figured that out yet from the number of pop-punk references in this book. And part of the magic of music is how it connects to our personal nervous system experience and cuts past our defenses. Pick one of your favorite songs. Pull up the lyrics to it, answer the following questions, and then listen to your song.

1. If your favorite song includes lyrics, write down the lyrics of the chorus below.

2. Play the chorus or a particularly arousing segment of your favorite song. Notice what sensations, feelings, and thoughts come up for you as you do. Write them below.

3. What, if any, nervous system state reactions come up for you? Write down which state reactions feel familiar.

As you might expect, our nervous systems have different reactions to different types of experiences, depending on which song you choose; you might repeat this exercise with the same song and have an entirely different experience and nervous system reaction. Feel free to do it again, with the same song and with others, and notice which songs bring you into your ventral state. You might want to keep a list of these calming songs (I've left a space for this below) and listen to them any time you need help entering a ventral state from a dorsal and/or sympathetic state.

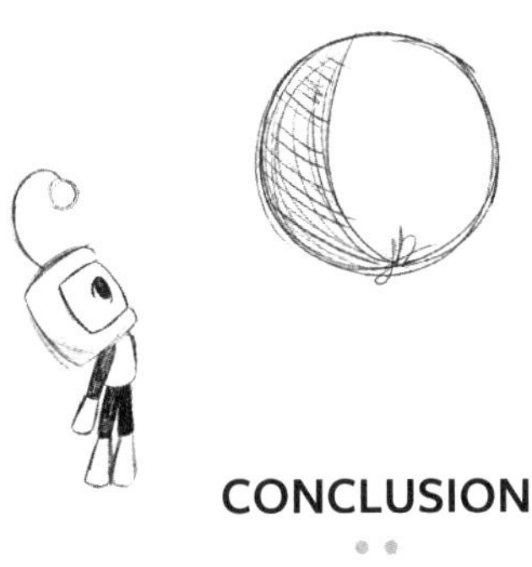

Cosmically Okay

The self cannot survive without love, and the self, starved of love, dies. The absence of self-love is shame, "just as cold is the absence of warmth."
—**FATHER GREGORY,** *TATTOOS ON THE HEART*

In November of 2024, I was invited to give a talk in Philadelphia, a place that is near and dear to my heart. From 2008 to 2012, I attended a small evangelical institution called Cairn University, which had a heavily Christian culture. As you might imagine, I did not and still do not fit in very well with what one might call "evangelical," but in the summer of 2010, I was invited by my creative writing professor, Susan, to her husband Gary's home church; and there I made friends with whom I'm still connected to more than a decade later. After giving this talk in Philadelphia in 2024, I had a chance to visit with Susan and Gary, and I shared with them how my life had been changing since the last time we had crossed paths, 5 years earlier.

As I shared about the woes of dating in my thirties and the joys of meeting influential people, Gary looked at me and said, "Sean, I'm really proud of you for meeting influencers and helping lots of people. But remember that even long before that, we were glad to know you, just as we're glad to know you now. You are cosmically okay." He was alluding to how he and Susan love me; that is, they accepted me long before I achieved anything or wrote any books. His point in telling me I'm "cosmically okay" (a reference to Father Gregory) was to indicate that my worth is independent of whether I'm accomplished. And so I share this story with you and the parts that make up your ever unfolding Autist Self to remind you that you, too, are cosmically okay.

COSMIC OKAYNESS AS AN INVITATION

I know this might not be easy to hear, but what if you are better than you believe you are? Consider the possibility that in your awkwardness and in your moments when you lack empathy, you inherently have both depth and worth. I think that for some, reading this may feel deeply dysregulating; in other words, as we've talked about in previous chapters, this validation may evoke a great deal of tension within you. But ultimately, I think vulnerability is for us, in all our Autist experiences, both disordering and nondisordering, moments of simultaneous tension and deep joy for the warmth of being seen and known.

And as much as you may hate hearing this, performing neural exercises and building vagal efficiency is really about culti-vating what Viktor Frankl called *the space between the stimulus and the response*. And it is in this magical middle ground that we find the endless possibility for freedom and connection that can only be known in the presence of the other or in relating to one-self. And so I invite you to consider taking a step into your own cosmic okayness. Take this opportunity for change, to assume not only the best about others but also about yourself, to see how deeply meaningful and wonderful you truly are, despite what you might believe about yourself at this given moment, because I know how hard it is to feel. To feel safe. Safe enough to be open again. Others may have hurt you. Not accepted you. Not invited you into the places you wanted to be or into the friendships you wanted to have.

Because it does hurt. Rejection sucks, and while it does, none of that rejection defines your Autist Self the way you might believe it does. Your Autist Self is deep and wonderful, and it holds more wisdom than you ever might know. And so, it is with this idea that I leave you: that despite what accomplishments you may have achieved, despite what failures or harms you may have caused, you are, indeed, cosmically okay. There is a Self both before and after this current Self of yours that is unfold-ing. The Self that is emerging can become more creative, more flexible, and more connected to themself and others. Through neural exercises like those presented in this book, I hope you find this version of yourself.

References

aan het Rot, M., Hogenelst, K. (2014). The influence of affective empathy and autism spectrum traits on empathic accuracy. *PLOS ONE, 9*(6), Article e98436. https://doi.org/10.1371/journal.pone.0098436

Alter, C. (2012, July 1). Motivational interviewing: A useful approach for families and counselors for post-secondary transitions. *Autism Spectrum News.* https://autismspectrumnews.org/motivational-interviewing-a-useful-approach-for-families-and-counselors-planning-for-post-secondary-transition/

American Psychiatric Association. (2013). *Diagnostic and statistical manual of mental disorders* (5th ed.).

American Psychiatric Association. (2022). *Diagnostic and statistical manual of mental disorders* (5th ed., Rev. ed.).

Anberlin. (2007). Dismantle. Repair [Song]. On *Cities*. Tooth and Nail Records.

Anderson, F. G. (n.d.). [as cited in] Roberts, D. (2022, January 3). *What is the Self in Internal Family Systems Therapy?* Dan Roberts. https://www.danroberts.com/blog/what-is-the-self-internal-family-systems

Anderson, L. K. (2023). Autistic experiences of applied behavior analysis. *Autism, 27*(3), 737–750. https://doi.org/10.1177/13623613221118216 https://doi.org/10.1177/13623613221118216

Asperger, H. (1944). Die "Autistischen Psychopathen" im Kindesalter [The "Autistic Psychopaths" in Childhood]. *Archiv für Psychiatrie und Nervenkrankheiten, 117*, 76–136.

REFERENCES

Bailey, R., Dugard, J., Smith, S. F., Porges, S. W. (2023). Appeasement: Replacing Stockholm syndrome as a definition of a survival strategy. *European Journal of Psychotraumatology, 14*(1), Article 2161038. https://doi.org/10.1080/20008066.2022.2161038

Barkley, R. A. (2012). *Executive functions: What they are, how they work, and why they evolved.* The Guilford Press.

Baron-Cohen, S. (1991). Precursors to a theory of mind: Understanding attention in others. In A. Whiten (Ed.), *Natural theories of mind: Evolution, development and simulation of everyday mindreading* (pp. 233–251). Basil Blackwell.

Barrett, S. L., Uljarević, M., Jones, C. R. G., & Leekam, S. R. (2018). Assessing subtypes of restricted and repetitive behaviour using the Adult Repetitive Behaviour Questionnaire-2 in Autistic adults. *Molecular Autism, 9,* 58. https://doi.org/10.1186/s13229-018-0242-4

Bell, R. (2017). *How to be here: A guide to creating a life worth living.* William Collins.

Bellesheim, K. R., Cole, L., Coury, D. L., Yin, L., Levy, S. E., Guinnee, M. A., Klatka, K., Malow, B. A., Katz, T., Taylor, J., & Sohl, K. (2018). Family-driven goals to improve care for children with autism spectrum disorder. *Pediatrics, 142*(3), e20173225.

Benevides, T., Carretta, H., & Lane, S. (2016). Unmet need for therapy among children with autism spectrum disorder: Results from the 2005–2006 and 2009–2010 national survey of children with special health care needs. *Maternal & Child Health Journal, 20*(4), 878–888. https://doi.org/10.1007/s10995-015-1876-x

Berdai, M. A., Labib, S., Chetouani, K., & Harandou, M. (2012). Atropa belladonna intoxication: A case report. *The Pan African Medical Journal, 11,* 72.

Bialik, M. (Host). (2024, March 19). Why bad boys feel good, with Dr. Stephen Porges! [Audio/video podcast]. *Bialik Breakdown.* www.bialikbreakdown.com/episodes/dr-stephen-porges

Billeci, L., Narzisi, A., Tonacci, A., Sbriscia-Fioretti, B., Serasini, L., Fulceri, F., Apicella, F., Sicca, F., Calderoni, S., & Muratori, F. (2017). An integrated EEG and eye-tracking approach for the study of responding and initiating joint attention in autism spectrum disorders. *Scientific Reports, 7*(1), Article 13560. https://doi.org/10.1038/s41598-017-13053-4

REFERENCES

Brand, S., Colledge, F., Ludyga, S., Emmenegger, R., Kalak, N., Sadeghi Bahmani, D., Holsboer-Trachsler, E., Pühse, U., & Gerber, M. (2018). Acute bouts of exercising improved mood, rumination and social interaction in inpatients with mental disorders. *Frontiers in Psychology, 9*, 249. https://doi.org/10.3389/fpsyg.2018.00249

Brenner, E. G., Schwartz, R. C., & Becker, C. (2023). Development of the internal family systems model: Honoring contributions from family systems therapies. *Family Process, 62*(4), 1290–1306. https://doi.org/10.1111/famp.12943

Bricout, V. A., Pace, M., Dumortier, L., Favre-Juvin, A., & Guinot, M. (2018). Autonomic responses to head-up tilt test in children with autism spectrum disorders. *Journal of Abnormal Child Psychology, 46*, 1121–1128. https://doi.org/10.1007/s10802-017-0339-9

Brookman-Frazee, L., Baker-Ericze, M., Stadnick, N., & Taylor, R. (2012). Parent perspectives on community mental health services for children with autism spectrum disorders. *Journal of Child and Family Studies, 21*(4), 533–544. https://doi.org/10.1007/s10826-011-9506-8

Byrne, E. A., Fleg, J. L., Vaitkevicius, P. V., Wright, J., & Porges, S. W. (1996). Role of aerobic capacity and body mass index in the age-associated decline in heart rate variability. *Journal of Applied Physiology, 81*(2), 743–750. https://doi.org/10.1152/jappl.1996.81.2.743

Campbell, T. S., Labelle, L. E., Bacon, S. L., Faris, P., & Carlson, L. E. (2012). Impact of mindfulness-based stress reduction (MBSR) on attention, rumination and resting blood pressure in women with cancer: A waitlist-controlled study. *Journal of Behavioral Medicine, 35*(3), 262–271. https://doi.org/10.1007/s10865-011-9357-1

Carnethon, M. R., Gulati, M., & Greenland, P. (2005). Prevalence and cardiovascular disease correlates of low cardiorespiratory fitness in adolescents and adults. *JAMA, 294*(23), 2981–2988. https://doi.org/10.1001/jama.294.23.2981

Cervantes, P. E., Conlon, G. R., Seag, D. E., Feder, M., Lang, Q., Meril, S., Baroni, A., Li, A., Hoagwood, K. E., & Horwitz, S. M. (2023). Mental health service availability for Autistic youth in New York City: An examination of the developmental disability and mental health service systems. *Autism, 27*(3), 704–713. https://doi.org/10.1177/13623613221112202

REFERENCES

Classen, C. C., Hughes, L., Clark, C., Hill Mohammed, B., Woods, P., & Beckett, B. (2021). A pilot RCT of a body-oriented group therapy for complex trauma survivors: An adaptation of sensorimotor psychotherapy. *Journal of Trauma and Dissociation, 22*(1), 52–68. https://doi.org/10.1080/15299732.2020.1760173

Corbett, B. A., Muscatello, R. A., & Baldinger, C. (2019). Comparing stress and arousal systems in response to different social contexts in children with ASD. *Biological Psychology, 140*, 119–30. https://doi.org/10.1016/j.biopsycho.2018.12.010

Dana, D. (2020) *Polyvagal Exercises for Safety and Connection: 50 client-centered practices*. W. W. Norton & Company.

Dana, D. (2021). *Anchored: How to befriend your nervous system using Polyvagal Theory*. Sounds True.

de Jong, R. K., Snoek, H., Staal, W. G., & Klip, H. (2019). The effect of patients' feedback on treatment outcome in a child and adolescent psychiatric sample: A randomized controlled trial. *European Child and Adolescent Psychiatry, 28*(6), 819–834. https://doi.org/10.1007/s00787-018-1247-4

Demers, L. A., Olson, E. A., Crowley, D. J., Rauch, S. L., & Rosso, I. M. (2015). Dorsal anterior cingulate thickness is related to alexithymia in childhood trauma-related PTSD. *PLOS ONE*, 10(10), e0139807.

Dickinson, E. (1894 volume of collected works). Letters. In M. Gold & P. Devine (Eds.), *The complete Emily Dickinson: A reader* (3rd ed., Vol. 47, pp. 265–284). Roberts Brothers. (Original work published 1884)

Dixon, E. M., Kamath, M. V., McCartney, N., & Fallen, E. L. (1992). Neural regulation of heart rate variability in endurance athletes and sedentary controls. *Cardiovascular Research, 26*(7), 713–719. https://doi.org/10.1093/cvr/26.7.713

Duncan, B. L., & Miller, S. D. (2000). The client's theory of change: Consulting the client in the integrative process. *Journal of Psychotherapy Integration, 10*(2), 169–187. https://doi.org/10.1023/A:1009448200244

Duncan, B. L., Miller, S. D., Sparks, J., & Claud, D. A. (2003). The Session Rating Scale: Preliminary psychometric properties of a "working" alliance measure. *Journal of Brief Therapy, 3*(1), 3–12.

Duncan, B. L., Miller, S. D., & Sparks, J. A. (2004). *The heroic client: A*

REFERENCES

revolutionary way to improve effectiveness through client-directed, outcome-informed therapy (Rev. ed.). Jossey-Bass.

Edmiston, E. K., Jones, R. M., & Corbett, B. A. (2016). Physiological response to social evaluative threat in adolescents with autism spectrum disorder. *Journal of Autism and Developmental Disorders, 46*, 2992–3005. https://doi.org/10.1007/s10803-016-2842-1

Erikson, E. H. (1950). *Childhood and society.* W. W. Norton & Company.

Eve, Z., Heyes, K., & Parry, S. (2023). Conceptualizing multiplicity spectrum experiences: A systematic review and thematic synthesis. *Clinical Psychology and Psychotherapy, 3*(1), e2910. https://doi.org/10.1002/cpp.2910

Franchini, M., Glaser, B., Wood de Wilde, H., Gentaz, E., Eliez, S., & Schaer, M. (2017). Social orienting and joint attention in preschoolers with autism spectrum disorders. *PLOS ONE, 12*(6), e0178859. https://doi.org/10.1371/journal.pone.0178859

Freitas, B. G. (2020). Questioning normativity: Exploring the experiences of Autistic adults who have undergone applied behavioural analysis (ABA) (Version 1). Toronto Metropolitan University. https://doi.org/10.32920/ryerson.14663727.v1

Furlan, R., Piazza, S., Dell'Orto, S., Gentile, E., Cerutti, S., Pagani, M., & Malliani, A. (1993). Early and late effects of exercise and athletic training on neural mechanisms controlling heart rate. *Cardiovascular Research, 27*(3), 482–488. https://doi.org/10.1093/cvr/27.3.482

Gallant, C., Roudbarani, F., Ibrahim, A., Maddox, B. B., & Weiss, J. A. (2023). Clinician knowledge, confidence, and treatment practices in their provision of psychotherapy to Autistic youth and youth with ADHD. *Journal of Autism and Developmental Disorders, 53*(11), 4214–4228. https://doi.org/10.1007/s10803-022-05722-9

Gerber, A. H., Nahmias, A., Schleider, J. L., & Lerner, M. D. (2024, June 4). Results from a pilot randomized controlled trial of a single-session growth-mindset intervention for internalizing symptoms in Autistic youth. *Journal of Autism and Developmental Disorders.* https://doi.org/10.1007/s10803-024-06341-2

Gerretsen, P., & Pollock, B. G. (2011). Rediscovering adverse anticholinergic effects. *Journal of Clinical Psychiatry, 72*(6), 869–870.

REFERENCES

Ghaderi, G., & Watson, S. L. (2019). "In medical school, you get far more training on medical stuff than developmental stuff": Perspectives on ASD from Ontario physicians. *Journal of Autism and Developmental Disorders, 49*(2), 683–691. https://doi.org/10.1007/s10803-018-3742-3

Gilmore, D. G., Longo, A., & Hand, B. N. (2022). The association between obesity and key health or psychosocial outcomes among Autistic adults: A systematic review. *Journal of Autism and Developmental Disorders, 52*(9), 4035–4043. https://doi.org/10.1007/s10803-021-05275-3

Goleman, D. (1987, March 10). Researcher reports progress against autism. *New York Times*, C1.

Golfenshtein, N., Srulovici, E., & Medoff-Cooper, B. (2016). Investigating parenting stress across pediatric health conditions—A systematic review. *Comprehensive Child & Adolescent Nursing, 39*(1), 41–79. https://doi.org/10.3109/01460862.2015.1078423

Gomez, S. (2016). Hands to Myself [Song]. On *Revival*. Interscope Records.

Goodman, B. (2016). Autonomic dysfunction in autism spectrum disorders (ASD) (P5. 117). *Neurology, 86*(16_Suppl.), 117. https://doi.org/10.1212/WNL.86.16_supplement.P5.117

Guy, L., Souders, M., Bradstreet, L., DeLussey, C., & Herrington, J. D. (2014). Brief report: Emotion regulation and respiratory sinus arrhythmia in autism spectrum disorder. *Journal of Autism and Developmental Disorders, 44*(10), 2614–2620. https://doi.org/10.1007/s10803-014-2124-8

Hacohen, N., Atzil-Slonim, D., Tuval-Mashiach, R., Bar-Kalifa, E., & Fisher, H. (2019). Multiplicity and mutuality in the transition of patient and therapist's self-states: Comparison of good vs. poor outcome groups. *Psychotherapy Research, 29*(6), 770–783. https://doi.org/10.1080/10503307.2017.1411625

Hartman, E., Schlegelmilch, A., Roskowski, M., Anderson, C. A., & Tansey, T. N. (2019). Early findings from the Wisconsin PROMISE Project: Implications for policy and practice. *Journal of Vocational Rehabilitation, 51*(2), 167–181.

Hector, B. (2024, June). Yesterday I posted about recognizing workplace ableism. Today, I am tackling what to do if it has already happened. *Being* [LinkedIn post]. https://www.linkedin.com/feed/update/urn:li:activity:7196117087918936065/

Heilman, K. J., Heinrich, S., Ackermann, M., Nix, E., & Kyuchukov, H.

REFERENCES

(2023). Effects of the safe and sound protocol (SSP) on sensory processing, digestive function and selective eating in children and adults with autism: A prospective single-arm study. *Journal on Developmental Disabilities, 28*(1), 1–26.

Heiss, S., Vaschillo, B., Vaschillo, E. G., Timko, C. A., & Hormes, J. M. (2021). Heart rate variability as a biobehavioral marker of diverse psychopathologies: A review and argument for an "ideal range." *Neuroscience and Biobehavioral Reviews, 121*, 144–155. https://doi.org/10.1016/j.neubiorev.2020.12.004

Hodgdon, H. B., Anderson, F. G., Southwell, E., Hrubec, W., & Schwartz, R. (2022). Internal family systems (IFS) therapy for posttraumatic stress disorder (PTSD) among survivors of multiple childhood trauma: A pilot effectiveness study. *Journal of Aggression, Maltreatment and Trauma, 31*(1), 22–43. https://doi.org/10.1080/10926771.2021.2013375

Hopper, A. (2023, March 3). *The meaning behind "Hands to myself" by Selena Gomez*. American Songwriter. https://americansongwriter.com/the-meaning-behind-hands-to-myself-by-selena-gomez/

Hwang, Y. I. J., Arnold, S., Srasuebkul, P., & Trollor, J. (2020). Understanding anxiety in adults on the autism spectrum: An investigation of its relationship with intolerance of uncertainty, sensory sensitivities and repetitive behaviours. *Autism, 24*(2), 411–422. https://doi.org/10.1177/1362361319868907

Inderbitzen, S. [@sensorimotor_psychotherapy]. (2024, April 2). *"SP provides me a way to experience feelings in a non-threatening way. Rather I experience them first through my body's"* Instagram. https://www.instagram.com/p/C5RLVH7RKwK/

Inderbitzen, S., & Porges, S.W. (2024). *Autism in polyvagal terms: New directions and possibilities*. W. W. Norton & Company.

Jensen, E. (2019, April 22). 5 takeaways on vulnerability from Brené Brown's "The call to courage." *USA Today*. https://www.usatoday.com/story/life/tv/2019/04/19/brene-brown-call-courage-netflix-vulnerability/3497969002/

Jonsdottir, S., Bouma, A., Sergeant, J. A., & Scherder, E. J. A. (2006). Relationships between neuropsychological measures of executive function and behavioral measures of ADHD symptoms and comorbid behavior.

REFERENCES

Archives of Clinical Neuropsychology, 21(5), 383–394. https://doi.org/10.1016/j.acn.2006.05.003

Jorba Galdos, L., & Warren, M. (2021). The body as cultural home: Exploring, embodying, and navigating the complexities of multiple identities. *Body, Movement and Dance in Psychotherapy, 17*(1), 81–97. https://doi.org/10.1080/17432979.2021.1996460

Kaminsky, L. A., Arena, R., Ellingsen, Ø., Harber, M. P., Myers, J., Ozemek, C., & Ross, R. (2019). Cardiorespiratory fitness and cardiovascular disease—The past, present, and future. *Progress in Cardiovascular Diseases, 62*(2), 86–93. https://doi.org/10.1016/j.pcad.2019.01.002

Kanner, L. (1968). Autistic disturbances of affective contact. *Acta Paedopsychiatrica, 35*(4), 100–136.

Keeley, R. D., Burke, B. L., Brody, D., Dimidjian, S., Engel, M., Emsermann, C., deGruy, F., Thomas, M., Moralez, E., Koester, S., & Kaplan, J. (2014). Training to use motivational interviewing techniques for depression: A cluster randomized trial. *Journal of the American Board of Family Medicine, 27*(5), 621–636. https://doi.org/10.3122/jabfm.2014.05.130324

Kerns, C. M., Rast, J. E., & Shattuck, P. T. (2020). Prevalence and correlates of caregiver-reported mental health conditions in youth with autism spectrum disorder in the United States. *Journal of Clinical Psychiatry, 82*(1), 20m13242. https://doi.org/10.4088/JCP.20m13242

Kinnaird, E., Stewart, C., & Tchanturia, K. (2019). Investigating alexithymia in autism: A systematic review and meta-analysis. *European Psychiatry, 55*, 80–89. https://doi.org/10.1016/j.eurpsy.2018.09.004

Kirsch, A. C., Huebner, A. R. S., Mehta, S. Q., Howie, F. R., Weaver, A. L., Myers, S. M., Voigt, R. G., & Katusic, S. K. (2020). Association of comorbid mood and anxiety disorders with autism spectrum disorder. *JAMA Pediatrics, 174*(1), 63–70. https://doi.org/10.1001/jamapediatrics.2019.4368

Klein, S. B., & Gangi, C. E. (2010). The multiplicity of self: Neuropsychological evidence and its implications for the self as a construct in psychological research. *Annals of the New York Acadamy of Sciences, 1191*(1), 1–15. https://doi.org/10.1111/j.1749-6632.2010.05441.x

Kodama, S., Saito, K., Tanaka, S., Maki, M., Yachi, Y., Asumi, M., Sugawara, A., Totsuka, K., Shimano, H., Ohashi, Y., Yamada, N., & Sone,

REFERENCES

H. (2009). Cardiorespiratory fitness as a quantitative predictor of all-cause mortality and cardiovascular events in healthy men and women: A meta-analysis. *JAMA*, *301*(19), 2024–2035. https://doi.org/10.1001/jama.2009.681

Kolacz, J., Kovacic, K., Dang, L., Li, B. U. K., Lewis, G. F., & Porges, S. W. (2023). Cardiac vagal regulation is impeded in children with cyclic vomiting syndrome. *The American Journal of Gastroenterology*, *118*(7), 1268–1275. https://doi.org/10.14309/ajg.0000000000002207

Kranz, S., Lukacs, J., Bishop, J., & Block, M. E. (2022). Intergeneration transfer of diet patterns? Parental self-report of diet and their report of their young adult children with ASD. *PLOS ONE*, *17*(2), Article 0263445. https://doi.org/10.1371/journal.pone.0263445

Kuo, A. A., Hotez, E., Rosenau, K. A., Gragnani, C., Fernandes, P., Haley, M., Rudolph, D., Croen, L. A., Massolo, M. L., Holmes, L. G., Shattuck, P., Shea, L., Wilson, R., Martinez-Agosto, J. A., Brown, H. M., Dwyer, P. S. R., Gassner, D. L., Kapp, S. K., Ne'eman, A., & Ryan, J. G. (2022). The Autism Intervention Research Network on Physical Health (AIR-P) research agenda. *Pediatrics*, *149*(Suppl. 4), e2020049437D. https://doi.org/10.1542/peds.2020-049437D

Kupferstein, H. (2018), Evidence of increased PTSD symptoms in Autistics exposed to applied behavior analysis. *Advances in Autism*, *4*(1), 19–29. https://doi.org/10.1108/AIA-08-2017-0016

Kurtz, R. (2009). *A course on the refined Hakomi method of mindfulness-based, assisted self-discovery* [Unpublished manuscript].

Kushki, A., Brian, J., Dupuis, A., & Anagnostou, E. (2014). Functional autonomic nervous system profile in children with autism spectrum disorder. *Molecular Autism*, *5*, Article 39. https://doi.org/10.1186/2040-2392-5-39

Laborde, S., Allen, M. S., Borges, U., Iskra, M., Zammit, N., You, M., Hosang, T., Mosley, E., & Dosseville, F. (2022). Psychophysiological effects of slow-paced breathing at six cycles per minute with or without heart rate variability biofeedback. *Psychophysiology*, *59*(1), e13952. https://doi.org/10.1111/psyp.13952

Lai, M. C., Kassee, C., Besney, R., Bonato, S., Hull, L., Mandy, W., Szatmari, P., & Ameis, S. H. (2019). Prevalence of co-occurring mental health diagnoses in the autism population: A systematic review and

REFERENCES

meta-analysis. *Lancet Psychiatry*, *6*(10), 819–829. https://doi.org/10.1016/S2215-0366(19)30289-5

Laugeson, E. A., Frankel, F., Mogil, C., & Dillon, A. R. (2009). Parent-assisted social skills training to improve friendships in teens with autism spectrum disorders. *Journal of autism and developmental disorders*, *39*(4), 596–606. https://doi.org/10.1007/s10803-008-0664-5

Lee, D.-C., Sui, X., Ortega, F. B., Kim, Y. S., Church, T. S., Winett, R. A., Ekelund, U., Katzmarzyk, P. T., & Blair, S. N. (2011). Comparisons of leisure-time physical activity and cardiorespiratory fitness as predictors of all-cause mortality in men and women. *British Journal of Sports Medicine*, *45*(6), 504–510. https://doi.org/10.1136/bjsm.2009.066209

Levinstein, K. (2018). Distorting psychology and science at the expense of joy: Human rights violations against human beings with autism via applied behavioral analysis. *Catalyst: A Social Justice Forum*, *8*(1), Article 5. https://trace.tennessee.edu/catalyst/vol8/iss1/5

Li, B., Blijd-Hoogewys, E., Stockmann, L., Vergari, I., & Rieffe, C. (2023). Toward feeling, understanding, and caring: The development of empathy in young Autistic children. *Autism*. *27*(5), 1204–1218. https://doi.org/10.1177/13623613221117955

Liang, X., Li, R., Wong, S. H. S., Sum, R. K. W., Wang, P., Yang, B., & Sit, C. H. P. (2022). The effects of exercise interventions on executive functions in children and adolescents with autism spectrum disorder: A systematic review and meta-analysis. *Sports Medicine*, *52*(1), 75–88. https://doi.org/10.1007/s40279-021-01545-3

Lieberman, J. A., III. (2004). Managing anticholinergic side effects. *The Primary Care Companion to the Journal of Clinical Psychiatry*, *6*(Suppl. 2), 20–23.

Lutfi, M. F., & Sukkar, M. Y. (2011). The effect of gender on heart rate variability in asthmatic and normal healthy adults. *International Journal of Health Science (Qassim)*, *5*(2), 146–154.

Maddox, B. B., Crabbe, S., Beidas, R. S., Brookman-Frazee, L., Cannuscio, C. C., Miller, J. S., Nicolaidis, C., & Mandell, D. S. (2020). "I wouldn't know where to start": Perspectives from clinicians, agency leaders, and Autistic adults on improving community mental health services for

Autistic adults. *Autism*, *24*(4), 919–930. https://doi.org/10.1177/136
2361319882227

Maddox, B. B., Crabbe, S. R., Fishman, J. M., Beidas, R. S., Miller, J. S., &
Mandell, D. S. (2019). Factors influencing the use of cognitive–behavioral
therapy with autistic adults: A survey of community mental health clinicians. Journal of Autism and Developmental Disorders, 49, 4421–4428.
https://doi.org/10.1007/s10803-019-04156-0

Maddox, B. B., Dickson, K. S., Stadnick, N. A., Mandell, D. S., & Brookman-
Frazee, L. (2021). Mental health services for aAutistic individuals across
the lifespan: Recent advances and current gaps. *Current Psychiatry
Reports*, *23*, Article 66. https://doi.org/10.1007/s11920-021-01278-0

Mayo Clinic. (2023, August 31). *Dissociative disorders*. Mayo Clinic.
https://www.mayoclinic.org/diseases-conditions/dissociative-disorders
/symptoms-causes/syc-20355215

McGill, O., & Robinson, A. (2021). "Recalling hidden harms": Autistic experiences of childhood applied behavioural analysis (ABA). *Advances in
Autism*, *7*(4), 269–282. https://doi.org/10.1108/AIA-04-2020-0025

Metzler, M., Duerr, S., Granata, R., Krismer, F., Robertson, D., & Wenning,
G. K. (2013). Neurogenic orthostatic hypotension: Pathophysiology, eval-
uation, and management. *Journal of Neurology, 260*, 2212–2219. https://
doi.org/10.1007/s00415-012-6736-7

Miller, J. G., Kahle, S., & Hastings, P. D. (2017). Moderate baseline vagal
tone predicts greater prosociality in children. *Developmental Psychology*,
53(2), 274–289. https://doi.org/10.1037/dev0000238

MINT. (n.d.). *About MINT: Motivational Interviewing Network of Trainers*.
Retrieved March 20, 2023, from https://motivationalinterviewing.org
/about_mint

Muscatello, R. A., Vandekar, S. N., & Corbett, B. A. (2021). Evidence for
decreased parasympathetic response to a novel peer interaction in older
children with autism spectrum disorder: A case-control study. *Journal
of Neurodevelopmental Disorders*, *13*, Article 6. https://doi.org/10.1186
/s11689-020-09354-x

Myers, J., Hadley, D., Oswald, U., Bruner, K., Kottman, W., Hsu, L., &
Dubach, P. (2007). Effects of exercise training on heart rate recovery

in patients with chronic heart failure. *American Heart Journal*, *153*(6), 1056–1063. https://doi.org/10.1016/j.ahj.2007.02.038

Nemiah, J. C., Freyberger, H., & Sifneos, P. E. (1976). Alexithymia: A view of the psychosomatic process. In O. W. Hill (Ed.), *Modern trends in psychosomatic medicine* (Vol. 3; pp. 430–439). Butterworths.

Neuhaus, E., Bernier, R., & Beauchaine, T. P. (2014). Brief report: Social skills, internalizing and externalizing symptoms, and respiratory sinus arrhythmia in autism. *Journal of Autism and Developmental Disorders*, *44*, 730–737. https://doi.org/10.1007/s10803-013-1923-7

New Focus Academy. (2020, September 21). What is motivational interviewing and how does it help teens on the spectrum? https://newfocusacademy.com/what-is-motivational-interviewing-and-how-does-it-help-teens-on-the-spectrum/

Nyström, P., Thorup, E., Bölte, S., & Falck-Ytter, T. (2019). Joint attention in infancy and the emergence of autism. *Biological Psychiatry*, *86*(8), 631–638. https://doi.org/10.1016/j.biopsych.2019.05.006

Ogden, P. (2021). *The pocket guide to sensorimotor psychotherapy in context.* W. W. Norton & Company.

Ogden, P., & Fisher, J. (2015). *Sensorimotor psychotherapy: Interventions for trauma and attachment.* W. W. Norton & Company.

Owens, A. P., Mathias, C. J., & Iodice, V. (2021). Autonomic dysfunction in autism spectrum disorder. *Frontiers in Integrative Neuroscience*, *15*, 787037. https://doi.org/10.3389/fnint.2021.787037

Oxford Languages. (n.d.). *Oxford languages and Google [English].* https://languages.oup.com/google-dictionary-en/

Pais, S. (2009). A systemic approach to the treatment of dissociative identity disorder. *Journal of Family Psychotherapy*, *20*(1), 72–88. https://doi.org/10.1080/08975350802716566

Park, J., Jun, J. Y., Lee, Y. J., Kim, S., Lee, S. H., Yoo, S. Y., & Kim, S. J. (2015). The association between alexithymia and posttraumatic stress symptoms following multiple exposures to traumatic events in North Korean refugees. *Journal of Psychosomatic Research*, *78*(1), 77–81.

Parks, M. (1985, February 11). Mandela rejects S. African terms for prison release. *Los Angeles Times.*

Parma, V., Cellini, N., Guy, L., McVey, A. J., Rump, K., Worley, J., Maddox,

REFERENCES

B. B., Bush, J., Bennett, A., Franklin, M., Miller, J. S., & Herrington, J. (2021). Profiles of autonomic activity in autism spectrum disorder with and without anxiety. *Journal of Autism and Developmental Disorders*, *51*(12), 4459–4470. https://doi.org/10.1007/s10803-020-04862-0

Parmentier, F. B. R., García-Toro, M., García-Campayo, J., Yañez, A. M., Andrés, P., & Gili, M. (2019). Mindfulness and symptoms of depression and anxiety in the general population: The mediating roles of worry, rumination, reappraisal and suppression. *Frontiers in Psychology*, *10*, 506. https://doi.org/10.3389/fpsyg.2019.00506

Patriquin, M. A., Hartwig, E. M., Friedman, B. H., Porges, S. W., & Scarpa, A. (2019). Autonomic response in autism spectrum disorder: Relationship to social and cognitive functioning. *Biological Psychology*, *145*, 185–197. https://doi.org/10.1016/j.biopsycho.2019.05.004

Pichot, V., Roche, F., Denis, C., Garet, M., Duverney, D., Costes, F., & Barthélémy, J. C. (2005). Interval training in elderly men increases both heart rate variability and baroreflex activity. *Clinical Autonomic Research*, *15*, 107–115. https://doi.org/10.1007/s10286-005-0251-1

Porges, S. W. (2017). *The pocket guide to Polyvagal Theory: The transformative power of feeling safe*. W. W. Norton & Company.

Porges, S. W. (2023). The vagal paradox: A polyvagal solution. *Comprehensive Psychoneuroendocrinology*, *16*, Article 100200. https://doi.org/10.1016/j.cpnec.2023.100200

Porges, S. W., Bazhenova, O. V., Bal, E., Carlson, N., Sorokin, Y., Heilman, K. J., . . . & Lewis, G. F. (2014). Reducing auditory hypersensitivities in Autistic spectrum disorder: Preliminary findings evaluating the listening project protocol. *Frontiers in Pediatrics, 2,* 80.

Porges, S. W., Macellaio, M., Stanfill, S. D., McCue, K., Lewis, G. F., Harden, E. R., Handelman, M., Denver, J., Bazhenova, O. V., & Heilman, K. J. (2013). Respiratory sinus arrhythmia and auditory processing in autism: Modifiable deficits of an integrated social engagement system? *International Journal of Psychophysiology*, *88*(3), 261–270. https://doi.org/10.1016/j.ijpsycho.2012.11.009

Prizant, B. M., Wetherby, A. M., Rubin, E., Laurent, A. C., & Rydell, P. J. (2006a). *The SCERTS Model: Vol. I. Assessment*. Brookes Publishing.

Prizant, B. M., Wetherby, A. M., Rubin, E., Laurent, A. C., & Rydell, P. J.

(2006b). *The SCERTS Model: Vol. II. Program planning and intervention.* Brookes Publishing.

PTSD UK. (2025, March 5). *Alexithymia and PTSD.* PTSDUK. https://www .ptsduk.org/alexithymia-and-ptsd/#:~:text=In%20the%20UK%2C%20 studies%20suggest,as%2085%25%20in%20some%20studies

Quinde-Zlibut, J. M., Williams, Z. J., Gerdes, M., Mash, L. E., Heflin, B. H., & Cascio, C. (2021). Multifaceted empathy differences in children and adults with autism. *Scientific Reports, 11*, Article 19503. https://doi .org/10.1038/s41598-021-98516-5

Ribáry, G., Lajtai, L., Demetrovics, Z., & Maraz, A. (2017). Multiplicity: An explorative interview study on personal experiences of people with multiple selves. *Frontiers in Psychology, 8*, 938. https://doi.org/10.3389 /fpsyg.2017.00938

Robinson, E. (n.d.). AZQuotes.com. Retrieved March 5, 2025, from https:// www.azquotes.com/quote/1527031?ref=lack-of-empathy

Rosenthal, S. B., Wilsey, H. R., Xu, Y., Mei, Y., Dea, J., Wang, S., Curtis, C., Sempou, E., Khokha, Mu. K., Chi, N. C., Willsey, A., J., Fisch, K. M., & Ideker, T. (2021). A convergent molecular network underlying autism and congenital heart disease. *Cell Systems, 12*. 1094–1107. https://doi .org/10.1016/j.cels.2021.07.009

Saito, I., Hitsumoto, S., Maruyama, K., Nishida, W., Eguchi, E., Kato, T., Kawamura, R., Takata, Y., Onuma, H., Osawa, H., & Tanigawa, T. (2015). Heart rate variability, insulin resistance, and insulin sensitivity in Japanese adults: The Toon health study. *Journal of Epidemiology, 25*(9) 583–591.

Sanchez, L. (2013, March 5). *Dr. Maya Angelou—I am human* [Video]. You-Tube. https://www.youtube.com/watch?v=ePodNjrVSsk

Sandercock, G. R., Bromley, P. D., & Brodie, D. A. (2005). Effects of exercise on heart rate variability: Inferences from meta-analysis. *Medicine and Science in Sports and Exercise, 37*(3), 433–439. https://doi.org/10 .1249/01.mss.0000155388.39002.9d

Schiepek, G. K., Stöger-Schmidinger, B., Aichhorn, W., Schöller, H., & Aas, B. (2016). Systemic case formulation, individualized process monitoring, and state dynamics in a case of dissociative identity disorder. *Frontiers in Psychology, 20*(7), Article 1545. https://doi.org/10.3389/fpsyg.2016 .01545

REFERENCES

Schwartz, J., & Brennan, B. (2013). *There's a part of me . . .* Trailheads Publications.

Schwartz, R. C. (1995). *Internal family systems therapy.* Guilford Press.

Schwartz, R. C. (2020). *No bad parts.* Sounds True.

Schwartz, R. C. (2023a). *Introduction to the internal family systems model.* Sounds True.

Schwartz, R. C. (2023b). *You are the one you've been waiting for: Bringing courageous love to intimate relationships.* Sounds True.

Sensorimotor Psychotherapy Institute. (2022) About. https://sensorimotor psychotherapy.org/about/#mission

Sensorimotor Psychotherapy Institute. (December, 2023). *Adaptive Strategies A primer for AIT ETZ.* At Sensorimotor Psychotherapy Institute level 3 training.

Sensorimotor Psychotherapy Institute. (December 2023). *Developmental Skills Consolidation Review# 2 AIT ETZ.* At Sensorimotor Psychotherapy Institute level 3 training

Sensorimotor Psychotherapy Institute. (December, 2023). PEACE Protocol. Pat Ogden, PhD. https://sensorimotorpsychotherapy.org/wp-content/ uploads/2022/07/SP-PEACE-PROTOCOLfor-Clients.pdf

Sharma, R. K., Balhara, Y. P., Sagar, R., Deepak, K. K., & Mehta, M. (2011). Heart rate variability study of childhood anxiety disorders. *Journal of Cardiovascular Disease Research, 2*(2), 115–122. https://doi.org/10 .4103/0975-3583.83040

Shi, H., & Hirai, M. (2024). Autistic traits linked to anxiety and dichotomous thinking: Sensory sensitivity and intolerance of uncertainty as mediators in non-clinical population. *Scientific Reports, 14,* Article 23334. https:// doi.org/10.1038/s41598-024-73628-w

Shields, G. S., Sazma, M. A., & Yonelinas, A. P. (2016). The effects of acute stress on core executive functions: A meta-analysis and comparison with cortisol. *Neuroscience and Biobehavioral Reviews, 68,* 651–668. https:// doi.org/10.1016/j.neubiorev.2016.06.038

Siegel, D. J. (2024a). *Personality and wholeness in therapy.* W. W. Norton & Company.

Siegel, D. J. (2024b, November 13). *Personality and wholeness in the cultivation of well-being* [Continuing education course presentation]. Maple Counseling.

REFERENCES

Sigrist, C., Mürner-Lavanchy, I., Peschel, S. K. V., Schmidt, S. J., Kaess, M., & Koenig, J. (2021). Early life maltreatment and resting-state heart rate variability: A systematic review and meta-analysis. *Neuroscience and Biobehavioral Reviews, 120*, 307–334. https://doi.org/10.1016/j.neubiorev.2020.10.026

Smeekens, I., Didden, R., & Verhoeven, E. W. (2015). Exploring the relationship of autonomic and endocrine activity with social functioning in adults with autism spectrum disorders. *Journal of Autism and Developmental Disorders, 45*, 495–505. https://doi.org/10.1007/s10803-013-1947-z

Soares-Miranda, L., Sandercock, G., Vale, S., Santos, R., Abreu, S., Moreira, C., & Mota, J. (2012). Metabolic syndrome, physical activity and cardiac autonomic function. *Diabetes/Metabolism Research and Reviews, 28*(4), 363–369.

Soares-Miranda, L., Sattelmair, J., Chaves, P., Duncan, G. E., Siscovick, D. S., Stein, P. K., & Mozaffarian, D. (2014). Physical activity and heart rate variability in older adults: The Cardiovascular Health Study. *Circulation, 129*(21), 2100–2110.

Sokol, J. T. (2009). Identity development throughout the lifetime: An examination of Eriksonian theory. *Graduate Journal of Counseling Psychology, 1*(2), Article 14. https://epublications.marquette.edu/cgi/viewcontent.cgi?article=1030&context=gjcp

Speer, K. E., Koenig, J., Telford, R. M., Olive, L. S., Mara, J. K., Semple, S., Naumovski, N., Telford, R. D., & McKune, A. J. (2021). Relationship between heart rate variability and body mass index: A cross-sectional study of preschool children. *Preventative Medicine Reports, 24*, Article 101638. https://doi.org/10.1016/j.pmedr.2021.101638

Speer, K. E., Naumovski, N., Semple, S., & McKune, A. J. (2019). Lifestyle modification for enhancing autonomic cardiac regulation in children: The role of exercise. *Children (Basel, Switzerland), 6*(11), 127. https://doi.org/10.3390/children6110127

Spek, A. A., van Ham, N. C., & Nyklíček, I. (2013). Mindfulness-based therapy in adults with an autism spectrum disorder: A randomized controlled trial. *Research in Developmental Disabilities, 34*(1), 246–253. https://doi.org/10.1016/j.ridd.2012.08.009

Stadnick, N. A., Lau, A. S., Dickson, K. S., Pesanti, K., Innes-Gomberg,

D., & Brookman-Frazee, L. (2020). Service use by youth with autism within a system-driven implementation of evidence-based practices in children's mental health services. *Autism, 24*(8), 2094–2103. https://doi.org/10.1177/1362361320934230

Stark, E., Stacey, J., Mandy, W., Kringelbach, M. L., Happé, F. (2021). Autistic cognition: Charting routes to anxiety. *Trends in Cognitive Sciences, 25*(7), 571–581. https://doi.org/10.1016/j.tics.2021.03.014

Suzuki, N., & Hirai, M. (2023). Autistic traits associated with dichotomic thinking mediated by intolerance of uncertainty. *Scientific Reports, 13*, 14049. https://doi.org/10.1038/s41598-023-41164-8

Székely, M. (2000). The vagus nerve in thermoregulation and energy metabolism. *Autonomic Neuroscience, 85*(1), 26–38. https://doi.org/10.1016/S1566-0702(00)00217-4

Tune, L. E. (2001). Anticholinergic effects of medication in elderly patients. *J Clin Psychiatry, 62*(Suppl. 21), 11–14.

Unigwe, S., Buckley, C., Crane, L., Kenny, L., Remington, A., & Pellicano, E. (2017). GPs' confidence in caring for their patients on the autism spectrum: An online self-report study. *The British Journal of General Practice, 67*(659), e445–e452. https://doi.org/10.3399/bjgp17X690449

van der Hart, O., Groenendijk, M., González, A., Mosquera, D., & Solomon, R. M. (2014). Dissociation of the personality and EMDR therapy in complex trauma-related disorders: Applications in phases 2 and 3 treatment. *Journal of EMDR Practice and Research, 8*, 33–48.

van der Kolk, B. A., & van der Hart, O. (1989). Pierre Janet and the breakdown of adaptation in psychological trauma. *American Journal of Psychiatry, 146*(12), 1530–1540. https://doi.org/10.1176/ajp.146.12.1530

Van Hecke, A. V., Lebow, J., Bal, E., Lamb, D., Harden, E., Kramer, A., Denver, J., Bazhenova, O., & Porges, S. W. (2009). Electroencephalogram and heart rate regulation to familiar and unfamiliar people in children with autism spectrum disorders. *Child Development, 80*(4), 1118–1133.

Van Sant, G. (Director). (1997). *Good Will Hunting.* Miramax.

Virani, S. S., Alonso, A., Benjamin, E. J., Bittencourt, M. S., Callaway, C. W., Carson, A. P., Chamberlain, A. M., Chang, A. R., Cheng, S., Delling, F. N., Djousse, L., Elkind, M. S. V., Ferguson, J. F., Fornage, M., Khan, S. S., Kissela, B. M., Knutson, K. L., Kwan, T. W., Lackland, . . . Tsao, C.

W. (2020). Heart disease and stroke statistics—2020 update: A report From the American Heart Association. *Circulation, 141*(9), e139–e596. https://doi.org/10.1161/CIR.0000000000000757

Virues-Ortega, J., Julio, F. M., & Pastor-Barriuso, R. (2013). The TEACCH program for children and adults with autism: A meta-analysis of intervention studies. *Clinical Psychology Review, 33*(8), 940–953. https://doi.org/10.1016/j.cpr.2013.07.005

Wampold, B. E., & Imel, Z. E. (2015). *The great psychotherapy debate: The evidence for what makes psychotherapy work* (2nd ed.). Routledge/Taylor and Francis Group.

Wang, H., Lu, Y., & Wang, Z. (2006). Function of cardiac M3 receptors. *Autonomic & Autacoid Pharmacology, 27*(1), 1–11. https://doi.org/10.1111/j.1474-8673.2006.00381.x

Ward, J. H., Weir, E., Allison, C., & Baron-Cohen, S. (2023). Increased rates of chronic physical health conditions across all organ systems in Autistic adolescents and adults. *Molecular Autism, 14*(1), 1–20. https://doi.org/10.1186/s13229-023-00565-2

Weiss, B. (2013). *Self-therapy workbook: An exercise book for the IFS process.* Pattern System Books.

Zahn, T. P., Rumsey, J. M., & Van Kammen, D. P. (1987). Autonomic nervous system activity in Autistic, schizophrenic, and normal men: Effects of stimulus significance. *Journal of Abnormal Psychology, 96*, 135–144. https://doi.org/10.1037/0021-843X.96.2.135

Zainal, N. Z., Booth, S., & Huppert, F. A. (2013). The efficacy of mindfulness-based stress reduction on mental health of breast cancer patients: A meta-analysis. *Psycho-Oncology, 22*(7), 1457–1465. https://doi.org/10.1002/pon.3171

Zammuto, M., Ottaviani, C., Laghi, F., & Lonigro, A. (2021). The heart in the mind: A systematic review and meta-analysis of the association between theory of mind and cardiac vagal tone. *Frontiers in Physiology, 12*, 611609. https://doi.org/10.3389/fphys.2021.611609

Index

Note: Italicized page locators refer to figures.

beliefs, parallel to nervous system states, 96, 103, 138

Bell, R., 127, 135

betrayal, relational context and dynamic of, 85

Big Bang Theory, The (television show), 27

biofeedback, 9, 31, 59

biofeedback plan example, 2023, 60–65

    biofeedback interventions, 61, 64

    frequency, 61, 65

    implementation period, 60, 64

    observations, 61–62, 65

    openness and organicity notes from, 62–63

    target flexibility goal, 60, 63

black-and-white thinking

    Autists and, 109

    description of, 108

body

    cognition shaped by, 138

    as a coping tool, 98

    as a naturally resourcing force, 75

    see also wisdom of the body

Body-Centered Psychotherapy (Kurtz), 117

body sensations

    describing your emotions and, 115

    favorite songs and, 151

    glimmers and, 135

    recalling a happy memory and, 76–78

    top-down wisdom and, 138

bottom-up processing, 14, 135

bottom-up wisdom, definition of, 29

breathing, biofeedback and, 59

Brompheniramine, increased heart beats per minute and, 22

Brown, B., 118

Cairn University, 155

calming songs, listing, 152–53

"Can't Keep My Hands to Myself" (Gomez), 120–21

capacity, expecting the worst and limited experience of, 97

cardiac activity

    alexythmia and elevated levels of, 70

    Autists and high levels of, 19–20, 34, 85, 93

    see also heart rate

Catholic church, splitting of, 30

celiac disease, increased heart beats per minute and, 22

change

    cosmic okayness and opportunity for, 157

    inability to cope with, 145

    personal responsibility, relational context, and, 85

    values applied with neural exercises and, 9

characteristics, strategies *vs.,* in ANE, 17

child part, fix-it part and, 106–7, 108/OG

Child Protective Services, 105, 107

see also acceptance; compassion; empathy; love
kind statement to yourself, writing, 45
Kinnaird, E., 69
Kurtz, R., 18, 117, 118

Latuda, increased heart beats per minute and, 22
Lauren, R., 6
Li, B., 39
"Like Gold" (Joy), 139
Lil Yachty, 49
lived experience, heightened cardiac activity and, 93
logic
    of feelings, 121
    pain and, 109
loneliness
    Autists and, 52–54
    neural exercises and decrease in, 58, 59
    pessimistic assumptions and, 102
    protective parts and, 54
    single session intervention on, study of, 53
    see also disconnection; isolation
Lovaas, O. I., 7
love, vulnerability and, 118. *see also* acceptance; compassion; connection; empathy; joy; kindness
love letter to my masked self, A (Garcia), xx
Love on the Spectrum (Netflix series), 56–58

low energy, dorsal elements and, 84
lozaril, increased heart beats per minute and, 22
Luther, Martin, 95 theses of, 30

Maddox, B., 127
maladaptive behaviors, 17, 18
managers, in Internal Family Systems model, 16, 17
Mandela, N., 146
Mapping Our Assumptions (Neural Exercise 10), 102–104
masking
    alexithymia as form of, 70
    defining, 50
    dorsal vagal activation and, 55
    example of, 51–52
    loneliness and, 52
    protectors and, 51
    see also alexithymia
Mate, G., 145
medical record, written by behavioral consultant, 79–81, 85
medications, heart rate variability and, 22–23
medulla oblongata, 54
memory
    dissociation and issues with, 37
    of intolerable times, change in, 140
    sense of safety and influence of, 142
mental flexibility, vagal efficiency and, 9
mental health care, uncertain access to, 127

Rot, 38

rumination, sympathetic activation and, 85

running, in biofeedback plan example, 61, 62

Sabbath, The (Heschel), 1

safe place, definition of, 71

safety, 31, 93, 119, 120

alleviation of alexithymia and felt sense of, 70

autonomic ladder and science of, *21*

cosmic okayness and, 157

cultivating, neuroscientific approaches to, 9

cultivating empathy through, 38–40

eliciting, by sharing feedback, 130–33

experiencing, PEACE protocol and, 97

glimmers and micromoments of, 133

memory and sense of, 142

organicity applied to, 123–24

Porges on, 6

relational context of, 79

vulnerability and baseline of, 123

see also felt sense of safety; neuroception; relational safety

Schwartz, A., 3

Schwartz, R. C.

parts theory of, xvi

the self as viewed by, 15–17, 22, 30

Self, the

adult, from a polyvagal perspective, 50–51

Anderson's description of, 50

ANE definition of, 16–18

Schwartz's view of, 2, 15–17, 30

Siegel's notion of, 1, 2, 8, 15, 30

traditional definitions of, departures from, 15–16

use of term, in text, 2, 15

self-loathing, moving beyond cycle of, 75

self-regulation, executive functioning and, 38

sensations, defining, 35–36. *see also* body sensations

sensation words, exploring, 115

Sensing from Your Nervous System (Neural Exercise 18), 150–53

Sensorimotor Psychotherapy (SP), 9, 31

ANE definition of Self and field of, 18

Core Organizers in, 29

neural exercises based on, 71

Sensorimotor Psychotherapy Institute website, original PEACE worksheet link, 98

sexual assault, 71

shame, masking and, 50

shutdown responses

dorsal system and, xviii, xix, 4–5, 19, *21,* 34, 37, 40

tension and rigidity and, 142

see also disconnection; numbness

About the Author

Sean M. Inderbitzen, DSW, LCSW, an Autist psychotherapist and researcher through the Mayo Clinic Health System resides in Rice Lake, WI, with his two sons. Sean is a clinical advisor to the AJ Autism Institute at Drexel University and the Autism Center for Sleep at Stanford University, and is an advisor to the Vanguard School in Malvern, PA. He regularly trains health care professionals to be more confident when working with people on the spectrum.